Praise for *Islam and Me*

"In this thought-provoking reflection on belonging, Fazel and Brioni make a powerful argument against damaging Eurocentric representations while demonstrating the generative antiracist capacity of collaborative knowledge."
—Heather Merrill, author of *Black Spaces: African Diaspora in Italy*

"Shirin Ramzanali Fazel narrates the daily life of diasporic Islam in Europe with deep lucidity and courage. This book shows that Islam has become the religion of European citizens, not just immigrants, and that diasporic Islam is a major test for European constitutional democracy."
—Amara Lakhous, author of *Divorce Islamic Style*

"Deftly blending self-reflection with critical analysis, Fazel and Brioni convincingly challenge the distorted representation of Islam in Europe by offering complex, unapologetic insights into Fazel's lived experiences as a Somali Italian Muslim woman."
—Maya Angela Smith, author of *Senegal Abroad: Linguistic Borders, Racial Formations, and Diasporic Imaginaries*

"Poetic and autobiographical, *Islam and Me* examines the intersection of media, memory, and language while questioning traditional models of knowledge. As a Muslim woman in one of the world's most distinctively Catholic countries, Fazel advocates for transnational belonging, and her witness is for everyone working towards more equitable societies today."
—Marie Orton, coeditor of *Contemporary Italian Diversity in Critical and Fictional Narratives*

Islam and Me

Titles in the **Other Voices of Italy** series:

# Other Voices of Italy: Italian and Transnational Texts in Translation

Editors: Alessandro Vettori, Sandra Waters, Eilis Kierans

This series presents texts in a variety of genres originally written in Italian. Much like the symbiotic relationship between the wolf and the raven, its principal aim is to introduce new or past authors—who have until now been marginalized—to an English-speaking readership. This series also highlights contemporary transnational authors, as well as writers who have never been translated or who are in need of a fresh/contemporary translation. The series further aims to increase the appreciation of translation as an art form that enhances the importance of cultural diversity.

This book is a meditation on the multireligious, multicultural, and multilingual reality of our time. It is a personal exploration of the necessity to rethink national culture and identity in a more diverse, inclusive, and antiracist way. Focusing specifically on the discrimination of Muslim women in Italy and the United Kingdom, Fazel looks at how this marginalized group is represented in Italian media. By questioning prevailing modes of representation, in the last portion of *Islam and Me: Narrating a Diaspora* the author argues that collaboration can be a way to avoid reproducing a colonial model of knowledge production, in which the white male scholar takes the work of an African female writer as an object of analysis.

# Islam and Me

~

## *Narrating a Diaspora*

SHIRIN RAMZANALI FAZEL

Edited by Simone Brioni

Translated by Simone Brioni
and Shirin Ramzanali Fazel

Rutgers University Press
New Brunswick, Camden, and Newark, New Jersey
London and Oxford

Rutgers University Press is a department of Rutgers, The State University of
New Jersey, one of the leading public research universities in the nation. By
publishing worldwide, it furthers the University's mission of dedication to
excellence in teaching, scholarship, research, and clinical care.

Library of Congress Cataloging-in-Publication Data
Names: Ramzanali Fazel, Shirin, author. | Brioni, Simone, editor, translator.
Title: Islam and me: narrating a diaspora / Shirin Ramzanali Fazel; edited by
Simone Brioni; translated by Simone Brioni and Shirin Ramzanali Fazel.
Other titles: Scrivere di Islam, raccontere la diaspora. English
Description: New Brunswick: Rutgers University Press, 2023. |
Series: Other voices of Italy | "Translation of Scrivere di Islam,
Raccontare la diaspora, Edizioni Cà Foscari, 2020." | Includes
bibliographical references and index.
Identifiers: LCCN 2022036707 | ISBN 9781978835825 (paperback) |
ISBN 9781978835832 (hardback) | ISBN 9781978835849 (epub) |
ISBN 9781978835856 (pdf)
Subjects: LCSH: Muslims—Non-Islamic countries. |
Islamophobia. | Cultural pluralism. | Sex discrimination against women. |
Immigrants' writings—History and criticism.
Classification: LCC BP52.5 .R3613 2023 |
DDC 305.6/97—dc23/eng/20220825
LC record available at https://lccn.loc.gov/2022036707

A British Cataloging-in-Publication record for this book is available
from the British Library.

References to internet websites (URLs) were accurate at the time of writing.
Neither the author nor Rutgers University Press is responsible for URLs that
may have expired or changed since the manuscript was prepared.

rutgersuniversitypress.org

# Contents

# Foreword

As Simone Brioni's introduction to the present work makes clear, what is sometimes referred to as the "transnational turn" in the way in which culture and society are approached and studied is now very firmly established. Part of the purpose of the body of scholarship that includes the works by such well-known figures as Arjun Appadurai (1996), Steven Vertovec (2009), Chiara De Cesari and Ann Rigney (2014), and Paul Jay (2010) is not, of course, to deny the role that nations perform in the way in which the world is organized both materially and conceptually, but to caution against the idea that the nation is a self-contained entity bound by one language and in which a set of homogeneous practices that define social interaction and institutional procedure can be easily identified. The wider purpose of this body of scholarship is to see the nation as a phenomenon that occurs within the transnational flow of economic, social, and cultural processes and is continually changing as a result of the often-hidden dynamism of those very processes. The value of a transnational approach in any one of its many articulations is that it allows one to see through some of the illusions that accompany the notion of the nation as a container of culture and to focus on the mobility of people and practices, on how cultures are in perpetual motion, and on how global interactions of the past and present create new realities while perpetuating deep and long-standing inequalities.

Within the context of what is broadly defined as Italian studies, a number of recent publications and projects have sought to develop a mode of scholarship that by looking at patterns of migration, at the evolution of economic exchange, and at the histories and manifold legacies of colonialism enables us to think about Italian culture in ways that are not bound by the nation-state.[1] A focus, for example, on migration opens inquiry into the functioning of communities in North and South America, in Australia, and across Europe and northern Africa, and throughout the Italian Peninsula itself. It encourages the examination of cultural and linguistic translation, of multiple forms of belonging, of everyday practices that are characterized not by their uniformity but by their very hybridity. Above all, the purpose of this mode of scholarship is to expose that the nature of what is referred to as Italian culture is permanently in flux, continually influenced by the flow of people between different parts of the world, by the ongoing energy of past processes of mobility.

It would be a great benefit to world economic sustainability if people were to think less about the borders of an individual nation-state, defined succinctly by Don Cupitt, as like "a rational egoist committed to living by a narrative of its own hard-won independence and steadily increasing wealth and power," and more about the web of interconnectivities that bind different parts of the world together and, against the background of impending climate catastrophe, upon which our common destiny depends (2015, 199). But notions about the homogeneity of national cultures persist and frequently give rise to acts of both verbal and physical violence. There is no end to the examples that one could indicate to prove this point, but the question of religion and, more specifically Islam, is highly relevant in this context.

The imperative behind the monograph that I published in 2016 was to examine some of the many ways in which both Islam and the Islamic world have been represented in Italy by journalists, writers, and cultural critics from the events of September 11, 2001, to the wave of Arab uprisings that followed on from the unrest in Tunisia after the death of Mohamed Bouazizi in 2011. The work set out to chart the rhetorical mechanisms and slippages of meaning that are characteristic of Islamophobic discourse at the same time as it attempted to show how such toxic uses of language have been counteracted by forms of writing that both have deconstructed the architecture of concepts on which antagonism toward Islam is based and have used highly inventive literary techniques to question biased modes of perception. The overall aim, as Brioni notes in the introduction to the present volume, was to consider the discursive environment that is continually being re-created with each new, widely disseminated intervention within the debate, an environment Italians live within and appropriate in diverse ways on a daily basis.[2]

There is no shortage of writings in Italy that have sought to disseminate a sinister image of Islam and to promote a vision of the West and the Islamic world as polar opposites, but it is worth isolating one current within this corpus that is of particular note because of the large circulation figures that it has attained.[3] Written by the extremely well-known journalist and author, Oriana Fallaci, and produced in the immediate aftermath of the attack on the World Trade Center, the trilogy, comprising the texts *La rabbia e l'orgoglio* (The rage and the pride) (2001), *La forza della ragione* (The force of reason) (2004a), and *Oriana Fallaci intervista sé stessa. L'Apocalisse* (Oriana Fallaci interviews herself. The Apocalypse) (2004b), became a publishing phenomenon of exceptional proportions.[4] This current of widely disseminated writing was continued in many of the books that Magdi—subsequently Magdi Cristiano—Allam produced in the latter years of the first decade of this century. Among the titles of the works that he published are *Grazie Gesù. La mia conversione dall'Islam al Cattolicesimo* (Thank you Jesus: My conversion from Islam to Catholicism) (2008) and *Europa Cristiana Libera: La mia vita tra verità e libertà, fede e ragione, valori e regole* (Free Christian Europe: My life between truth and freedom, faith and reason, values and rules) (2009).[5] More recently, figures who occupy a prominent position in the public eye like the journalist and editor in chief of the right-wing national daily *Libero*, Vittorio Feltri, have ensured the continuation of this vein of journalistic production with the publication of texts like *Non abbiamo abbastanza paura: noi e L'Islam* (We don't have enough fear: Islam and us) (2015).

This is not the space to analyze these texts in detail, but it is worth isolating some of the features that characterize the form that the writing assumes and the discourse that it constructs. All these works share a number of formal characteristics: they are written in the first person, include many incidents drawn from the experiences of their writer, and often use the subjective reactions of their author to particular incidents or phenomena as a means of suggesting responses that, they argue, should be adopted collectively. More important than the formal similarities that exist between the texts are the arguments that they construct in order to advocate opposition to Islam. Each argument is inevitably enmeshed with another, but it is useful to indicate some of the key elements that have characterized this form of writing with its evident intention to stimulate a series of reactions in its extensive readership.

The most significant element of this body of writing is that it does not insist on the distinction between Islamist extremism and Islam as a religion and culture. The conception of Islam that is present throughout Fallaci's trilogy and is set forth explicitly in the preface to *La rabbia e l'orgoglio* is that, as a religion and as a civilization, it represents an unmoving body of thought and belief that structures human identity in such a way that it is relentlessly hostile to the West. What the trilogy does is to argue that fundamentalism is not a separate reality, divorced from the central current of Islam, but the expression of the inner form of the Muslim world. Instead of representing a deeply heterogeneous reality, Fallaci constructs an image of the Islamic world as a homogenized totality. The trilogy not only collapses distinctions between different parts of the Muslim world but sees every Muslim as the product of a radical version of Islam and, as a consequence, complicit in the furthering of a violent, anti-Western ideology.

It is an interesting fact that in his text of 2005, *Vincere la paura*, Magdi Allam was highly critical of the thesis that Fallaci propounded in *La rabbia e l'orgoglio*. He accused Fallaci of speaking of a reality to which she was extraneous and of failing to place either herself or her culture in discussion. By contrast, he used what he referred to as his exceptional personal circumstances as a means of deconstructing a stereotype of Muslims and of modern Islamic culture. He asserted the multifaceted and exclusive nature of his own lived experience and offered a testimony of his own life story.[6] Whereas Fallaci's trilogy interprets history as a cyclical process in which the threat of fundamentalist terror is equated with the earlier menace of fascism and bolshevism, Allam's evocation of his childhood growing up in Egypt charted the progress of a history that does not obey a determinist logic. He insisted on the multiethnic and multiconfessional nature of all civilizations and described Islam as sharing with the West an intrinsic cultural contamination that is subject to its own evolution (Allam 2008, 134). However, while in his earlier writing he argued against the danger of conflating the whole of the Muslim world with radical Islamism, his later texts elaborated an altogether different interpretation of Islam. In both *Grazie Gesù* and *Europa Cristiana Libera* he claimed that his own endeavors to argue for the recognition of an Islam that is free from fundamentalism led him to an understanding that, while there may be "moderate Muslims," there is no such thing as a "moderate Islam." His writing has maintained that the "incitement to hatred" and the "instigation of violence" are not limited to a radical, ideological interpretation of Islam but are integral to the religion itself.[7]

If the conflation of Islamist extremism with Islam as a whole is one element that characterizes this body of writing, then another is the articulation of a belief that a conspiracy to undermine the West is well advanced. In *La forza della ragione* Fallaci argues that the increase in the numbers of Muslims living in Western Europe is not simply the effect of migratory flows determined mostly by global economic factors but the result of deliberate Islamic expansionism. Fallaci not only claims that Western governments have failed to resist what she sees as the surreptitious Islamification of Europe but also maintains that, blinded by the necessity of importing crude oil, they have connived in the process over decades and that they are therefore guilty of what she terms the sale of Western identity. Like so much of the trilogy, the theory that is advanced is based on very little formal documentation, yet it is used to substantiate one of Fallaci's most disturbing propositions. She does not simply maintain, to use Samuel P. Huntington's (1997) concept, that there is a "clash of civilizations" between Islam and the West: her assertion is rather that it is the aim of the Islamic world to undermine and colonize Western societies by changing their demographics and by undermining their systems of value.

In *Non abbiamo abbastanza paura*, Vittorio Feltri (2015) sees himself as someone who is prepared to voice sentiments that others lack the foresight or the courage to state publicly. The purpose of his work, as is made clear from its opening pages, is to carry forward the campaign that Fallaci had initiated, and the book does not, therefore, add substantially to the ideas that are present in the trilogy. Instead of seeing Islam as a complex that has built up over centuries with remarkably different traditions and forms of adherence, Feltri—like Fallaci—sees Islam as a homogenic totality and draws little or no distinction between different currents within Islamic thought and practice.[8] He sees the Quran as a text that seeks to inspire an aggressive attitude toward everything that it considers other, and developing an assertion that is present in the trilogy, he draws an analogy between Islam and totalitarianism.[9] He espouses the notion of there being an Islamic conspiracy to undermine the West, and taking up a metaphor that is deployed extensively in the trilogy, he refers to Troy being under siege and Fallaci as a latter-day Cassandra. Still more closely aligned to the thesis that is propounded by the trilogy, he contends that the West—by failing to recognize that a "war of religions" or an "invasion" is happening and by promoting a multicultural vision rather than a robust definition of its own values—will prove complicit in its own decline.

Though it is true that Feltri's intervention does not present much that is new—at least in terms of content—to the texts that both Fallaci and Allam have produced, his book is useful in revealing an essential component of this body of writing, namely its intention to provoke strong emotional reactions. Any academic study will immediately reveal how the writing as a whole avoids engagement with recognized scholarship in favor of an appeal to the supposed common sense of its readership;[10] how reference to Italy's long-standing former colonial engagement in Muslim-majority countries (including Eritrea, Libya, and Somalia) is almost entirely lacking despite what most people would regard as its obvious relevance; how theoretical discussion of the meaning of such terms as "culture," "society," and "subjectivity" is shunned in favor of a reliance on what is posited as the self-evident and essentialist meaning of these terms.[11]

It is no doubt true that works of the kind that I have selected have played a significant part in public debate concerning the question of Italy's relationship with Islam and the Islamic world in the first two decades of this century. Owing to the status of figures like Fallaci, Allam, and Feltri as well-known journalists, views expressed in their writings have received significant media coverage; they have been reflected in the rhetoric of political parties;[12] and they have impacted people's everyday consciousness of the nature of Italy's identity, its likely future development, and its place within global geopolitics. It is also of course true that many of the propositions that are at the center of this body of work have been subject to profound analysis and contestation by academics, journalists, writers, and established figures belonging to a range of religious communities.

A number of Italy's leading journalists, including Lilli Gruber, Maurizio Molinari, and Domenico Quirico, have produced book-length studies that combine the firsthand observation of the reality of some of the world's most dangerous conflict zones with lengthy analyses of the conceptual issues that underlie both actual and potential incidents of intercommunal violence.[13] Within the academic community, numerous studies have appeared that examine the question of Islamist extremism while deliberately setting out to explore what we mean when we talk about religion or culture and how our own habits of inference and deduction need continuously to be exposed to scrutiny.[14] Sociologist Stefano Allievi wrote an alternative trilogy to Fallaci's works shortly after they appeared, arguing that her ideas needed to be refuted with the kind of direct, personal, and accessible style that characterized her writing (2006, 17–18). Above all, his response concentrated on what he defined as the "poisonous, shameful, and unworthy" (2006, 53) assertion that there is a connecting line between Islamic fundamentalism and migration to Italy, and how such an assertion all too easily translates into acts of violence and discrimination against Italy's Muslim population.[15] Similarly, the late Algerian-born sociologist Khaled Fouad Allam wrote a number of works on the Islamic world and on Islam within Italy (2004, 2011). His most well-known text, *L'Islam spiegato ai Leghisti* (Islam explained to members of the Northern League) (2011), sought to examine the thinking of the Lega Nord on Islam and on migration; it considered the various facets of Islamophobia, the wider context of Islam's relation with the West, and the growing evidence of Islam's presence in Italy as the country's second religion.

Within the field of literary communication, writers such as Amara Lakhous and Randa Ghazy have used the novel as a means both of bringing the effects of Islamophobia to public awareness and of investigating how people who share the same space but who are from separate communities view one another, how their perceptions are to varying degrees

determined by preconceived ideas, and how these perceptions are in turn complicated by emotional entanglements
of various kinds. Distinguished by its wealth of intertextual
reference and by its cultivation of a polyphonous form of narration, Lakhous's novel of 2010, *Divorzio all'islamica a viale
Marconi* (*Divorce Islamic Style*), addresses how feelings of
suspicion and distrust are threaded into perceptions of Italy's
Muslim population. Ghazy's fictional autobiography, *Oggi
forse non ammazzo nessuno: storie minime di una giovane musulmana stranamente non terrorista* (Today perhaps I won't kill
anyone: Minimal stories of a young Muslim who is strangely
not a terrorist), was published in 2007.[16] In the text, Jasmine,
the twenty-three-year-old Italo-Egyptian narrator, finds herself continually confronted with a stereotypical image of her
own identity and the consequential necessity of defending
who she believes herself to be. The act of defending who she
is in a series of everyday interactions with other people
encourages, at one level, a longing for an identity that is less
complex, while at another more profound level it leads her to
develop a fully conscious understanding of the daily molding
of her subjectivity.

In his text, *Lettere contro la guerra* (Letters against
war), itself written as a response to Fallaci's *La rabbia e
l'orgoglio*, Tiziano Terzani argued that the events of September 11, 2001, and the global chain of events that they set in
motion imposed upon everyone an intimidating series of
injunctions. In the view that he elaborated in each of the "letters" of his collection, the reality horrifically inaugurated by
9/11 imposes the need always to interrogate the frame in
which our judgments and assumptions are based; to consider
the extent to which we see ourselves as living within
national or at least geographically situated traditions; to be
more alive to the transnational or transcultural dimension

of human experience; and, above all, to be aware of the extreme inequalities that are perpetuated by the ongoing development of deeply laid historical processes. The primary function of all of the works to which I have briefly alluded is to allow the reader to expand their consciousness by exploring how local and specific settings are ultimately intelligible only when placed in more global structures and how the world appears in its everyday, polyrhythmic, and multidirectional functioning from diverse perspectives.

Shirin Ramzanali Fazel's text clearly belongs to the body of creative and autobiographical writing that I have isolated. It engages directly with an identifiable corpus of representations that express aversion toward Islam and the extensive media coverage that that corpus has received. It examines in intricate detail the positionality from which its author sees the world both as it appears in its changing cultural frameworks and as it is experienced through quotidian contacts with people in private and public settings, through bureaucratic encounters, and through instances of travel and displacement. It invites its reader to participate in a personal inquiry into how faith is experienced and how subjectivity, the person's ongoing construction and performance of their sense of selfhood, is always relational, intertwined with the consciousness of significant others, dependent on linguistic structures, and receptive to the properties of specific localities.

As is indicated by its title, *Islam and Me* is an inquiry into how faith is experienced and how the individual understands the practice of religion, Islam's ethics-led approach to life and its sacred understanding of the world, the meaning of prayer, the unmediated relationship to God. The text is an inquiry into the societal contexts in which religion is experienced; it discusses communities of worship in different parts of the globe and how they are shaken by examples of Islamist extremism. Above all, it explores the mechanics of Islamophobia, more properly defined as anti-Muslim discrimination or racism.[17] It looks at the frameworks that are habitually relied upon by the media, their tendency to place representatives of different communities in opposition to one another, to insist on a certain intellectual simplicity, and to apply labels to human beings. It gives instances of how distortions concerning the nature and history of Islam seep into different elements of society, from political discourse to children's textbooks. It considers the psychological power of words and how the collective imaginary is dynamic, willing to use emotion as a mode of cognition, and easily susceptible to rhetoric. Throughout, it sees a given societal context as contingent, liable to change, and understandable only in terms of comparison or contrast with other sites that, though apparently distinct and in many instances thousands of miles apart, are connected through the movement of people over centuries and by the gradual sedimentation of cultural traditions.

Rather than offering a dispassionate analysis of the forces that are at play in the way in which people attempt to lead their lives amid shifting cultural and social coordinates, the text is an exploration of how a given societal context is experienced from the positionality of a Muslim woman whose life has been, and is, lived in a variety of settings in different parts of the world. It sees events and situations from the perspective of those who are discriminated against. It asks what you go through when your sense of yourself, your gender, and your relationship with other people is jolted by what you witness both in the public sphere and in specific surroundings; what happens when identities with which you are unfamiliar are foisted upon you; what happens when you are routinely asked invasive questions and when you are suddenly made aware of the material constraints that borders impose. As

Shirin writes, "Sometimes I've been discriminated against because of my veil, sometimes I've talked to victims of discrimination, sometimes I've read their stories and tried to ask myself how I would feel and what I would have done if I had been in their place. I've tried to collect their voices and their stories by reporting them as they were told to me or by trying to reconstruct them from my perspective" (68). Yet underlying the registration of the effects that lived or reported incidents create in the mind and the emotions of the author lies the narrative structure of the text. The current of connected meaning that runs through the book is to be found both in the circumstances that are recounted and in the nature of the response that is elaborated by the author. At the heart of the book lies a dialogic configuration: it is true that one sees the world from a determined positionality, but it is also true that the world of external appearances illuminates that positionality. It is by delving deeper into one's subjectivity, by interpreting how the sounds of others' voices resonate within your consciousness, and by interrogating the interface between the public and the private that you attain a level of perception that enables you to identify the pressures that act upon your sense of self and those of other people, to deconstruct the nature of their operation, and at least in part to divest them of the power that they seek to impose.

One of the dimensions of collective and individual life that is most powerfully brought into focus by the author's mode of inquiry relates to the experience of time. Though the voice of the author is positioned in the here and now, the present is seen not as the ground in which we situate all our experiences but more as the vantage point from which we can see the merging of the past into the future. Acts of discrimination that are witnessed either in person or through the media are interpreted as visible indications of long-standing and continuing processes that separate human beings according to entrenched notions of similarity or difference. Sustaining the text as a whole is the argument that we need to be aware that perception is only partially independent and that we need to interrogate our habitual attributions of meaning to the realities that surround us. A substantial part of a more interrogative stance toward ourselves and the world that we inhabit lies in resisting the temptation to see culturally located traditions as universally applicable models of behavior. When writing on the statements that are frequently made by Western politicians on the need to "liberate" Muslim women from restrictions regarding dress and conduct, Shirin declares, "Such statements are made without considering the women they are addressing: they have brains, spirituality, and great respect for themselves. Our so-called liberation would mean forcing us to strip ourselves and adopt a model of morality and femininity that we do not share. I also want to point out that this approach has something paternalistic about it, typical of the period of colonial domination, during which it was necessary to 'teach' the submissive how to behave in a 'civilized' manner" (56). As is argued in this short extract and indeed throughout the book, the manifold legacies of colonialism exercise both a direct influence on the way in which the world is organized and an unseen power in the way in which contemporary attitudes are formulated. It is only by seeking to untangle how the past is woven into the fabric of the present that one can begin to avoid some of the seductive simplifications that see practices and people confined within the lines that are traced by officially sanctioned borders. Movements, as they occur both spatially and temporally, are multidirectional, as is evidenced with singular clarity by the author when she speaks about the depth of her involvement with the moving body of histories, practices, and identifications that constitutes what is referred to by the more than imperfect expression "Italian culture." It makes no sense for her to claim that the circumstances of her life have taken her to Italy and that the affinity that she feels with the country is motivated by volition when historically and culturally speaking: "It was Italy that first came to me. It had come into my hometown of Mogadishu, and I was crossed by that border" (2).

The depth with which Shirin Ramzanali Fazel is grappling with issues that are deeply embedded within her subjectivity is reflected in the form that the work assumes. The fluidity with which circumstances in the present initiate incursions into personal and generational memory indicates not simply how the act of remembering draws from a stable repository of the past but how that repository is susceptible to the nature of the ongoing experiences of the person who remembers.[18] The fluidity of the interchange between the experiences of different moments of the author's understanding of her relation to the world of external reality is accompanied—as it has to be if it is to translate the different keys in which memory communicates—by frequent changes in register, by sudden movements between prose and poetry, and by varying ways of addressing the reader. The variation of the author's mode of address is lent an additional level of intricacy by the nature of the collaboration with Simone Brioni. The text is arguing throughout for a breakdown in any traditional separation between writing and criticism; it is suggesting that dialogue between critic and writer can and should be built into the nature of the work, all the more so if that work is actively seeking not only to comment on but to intervene in social processes and changes.

One of the most striking features of the text is its desire to involve the reader in the emotional and epistemological experiences of the author. In part that impulse derives from the nature of the question that is being considered; if we are to avoid the mistaken perception that people live within disconnected and incommensurate realities, then an exploration and a sharing of the influences that play upon one's cultural, religious, and social identity is necessary and writing that performs this kind of work is of undeniable value. But in a world in which we face the ongoing threat of Islamist extremism and the analogous menace of xenophobic popular nationalism, then that work becomes all the more important. A recurring thematic feature of the text is the need to develop an awareness of our present realities that is alive to the unthinking perpetuation of past injustices. It is also true that the text is arguing that uncompromising attitudes to what is perceived as different are "harbingers of future calamities" (32), and the dialogue on how we attempt to anticipate the future is central to the reading experience of *Islam and Me*.

Charles Burdett
Institute of Languages, Cultures and Societies,
School of Advanced Study,
University of London

# An Introduction
## to a *Meticcio* Text

This introduction delineates a critical and historical context within which *Islam and Me* can be read. I am writing this text as a scholar of migration literature in Italian, and as Shirin's interlocutor and collaborator in the production of *Islam and Me*. Indeed, this volume has emerged from Shirin's reflections on Islamophobia and from our dialogue about our own collaboration, Italian postcolonial literature, the legacy and memory of colonialism, and the presence of racism and religious discrimination in Italy. The use of the adjective *meticcio* to identify this volume aims to emphasize its hybrid and collaborative nature and its antiracist purpose. *Meticcio* literally means mestizo or mixed-race in Italian, but it can be also used with a more figurative and abstract meaning to indicate cross-cultural creolization and braiding. This is a *meticcio* text because it is the result of what Françoise Lionnet calls *métissage*, namely a cultural crosspollination, "a concept and a practice . . . the site of undecidability and indeterminacy, where solidarity becomes the fundamental principle of political action against hegemonic languages" (1989, 6).

While this text is an example and a celebration of *meticciato*, the term *meticcio* was employed, in a derogatory way, during colonial times to denote mixed-raced people who were not recognized as belonging to the "superior Italian race." Indeed, mixed-race interactions played an important role in the history of Italian colonialism in Somalia, Shirin's home country. Somalia was an Italian protectorate from 1885 to 1905; it then became a colony, and it was part of the Italian Empire from 1935 until the end of the Second World War. The Italian Empire in Africa included Libya, Eritrea, and Ethiopia (Del Boca 1976–1984; Labanca 2002). In 1934, when Libya became a unified Italian colony, Mussolini decided to assume the title of Protector of Islam in order to create alliances against France and the United Kingdom, despite the fact that he had signed the Lateran Treaty with the Catholic Church in 1929. John Wright argues that this decision sprang from political opportunism: "The rapid conquest of the Ethiopian empire in 1935–1936 had brought many more Muslims under Italian rule: those of Eritrea, Somalia, Libya, and Ethiopia were by 1936 estimated at about nine million. Italy had thus become a leading 'Muslim' power, conscious that her imperial record provided a means of enhancing or damaging her standing in Islamic opinion everywhere, but most particularly in the increasingly nationalistic Arab world" (2010, 125). I believe that this point is significant, as Italian neofascist parties often discriminate against Muslim immigrants by referring to Europe's alleged "Christianity," thereby concealing this rather unknown, yet fundamental part of Italian history. It is equally important to point out that Italians committed the largest mass murder of Christians in Africa, namely the 1937 Yekatit 12 extermination. Yekatit 12 coincides with February 19 on the Gregorian calendar. On this day, almost 20 percent of Addis Ababa's entire population—19,200 people—were killed in Debre Libanos, Ethiopia, in retaliation for the failed assassination attempt on a fascist official, General Rodolfo Graziani (Campbell 2017).

Despite the numerous crimes committed by Italians in their colonies, from 1950 to 1960 the United Nations entrusted the management of Somalia (Amministrazione Fiduciaria Italiana della Somalia, AFIS) to the former colonizers, a unique case in the process of decolonization (Morone 2011; Tripodi 1999, 106–137). AFIS was a de facto continuation of colonial rule, during which time the Italian government questionably gave the former fascist administration the duty of guiding this African country to independence and democracy.

The decision to give Italy this political responsibility was controversial given that during colonialism Italians implemented a form of apartheid in their colonies, thanks to law 1019 of 1936, which denied mixed-race people rights of citizenship, and to law 880 of 1937, which penalized interracial relationships with a five-year prison sentence (Giuliani 2018, 65–108). Italy also implemented systematic segregation measures thanks to the 1938 racial laws. Discrimination against mixed-race individuals in colonial society had long-lasting effects both in the former colonies (Morone 2018) and in the Italian collective imagery (Comberiati 2018).

While *meticciato* was forbidden in the colonies in the late 1930s (Giuliani Caponetto 2015), the adjective *meticcio* has recently been reappropriated to indicate antiracist collaborations. For instance, this term is used in the title of Wu Ming 2 (Giovanni Cattabriga) and Antar Mohamed's *Timira. Romanzo meticcio* (Timira. A *meticcio* novel). The novel recounts the story of the Somali Italian actress Isabella Marincola and aids in the understanding of the colonial legacy in both Italy and Somalia. A passage from the book reads, "Stories belong to everybody—they emerge from a community and are returned to a community—even when they take the form of autobiography and seem to belong to an individual" (2012, 503). Regarding this quote, I claimed elsewhere that "'meticcio' collaborations . . . are a mediation between different perspectives on History, and they can help redefine the concept of national belonging and reclaiming rights for those people who would like to be considered Italians regardless of the color of their skin" (Brioni 2013a, 114). *Islam and Me* is a *meticcio* volume: it is the result of a collaboration between a writer and a scholar and includes personal and collaborative reflections, which we hope can contribute to the emergence of collective narratives and memories about the colonial legacy and the discrimination of Muslims within Italy and beyond.

## Shirin Ramzanali Fazel's Life and Work

Shirin Ramzanali Fazel is an Italian writer of Somali and Pakistani origin. She was born in Mogadishu in 1953, during Somalia's Italian trusteeship, and as a child she attended Italian schools in the Somali capital city. In 1971 she moved to Italy, where she lived for periods until 1996—in Novara from 1971 to 1976 and in the Vicenza area from 1985 to 1986 and again from 1989 to 1996. She also resided in Lusaka (Zambia, 1976–1978), Jeddah (Saudi Arabia, 1978–1984), and New York (United States, 1986–1989). From 1996 to 2004, Shirin lived in Kenya, before returning to Italy, and then moving to Birmingham, England, in 2010. Although Shirin now lives in the United Kingdom, she has maintained strong ties with Italy and goes often to Carmignano di Brenta, a village in the province of Padua, where she lived from 2005 to 2010 and where one of her daughters currently resides.

Shirin's first novel, *Lontano da Mogadiscio*, describes the author's experience of migration and the legacy of Italian colonialism in her country of origin. I emphasize elsewhere this novel's contribution to "decolonizing the Italian collective memory, testifying to a Black person's experience in Italy from the seventies to the nineties . . . , and [to preserving] the memory of . . . Mogadishu [before its destruction during] a devastating civil war beginning in 1991" (Brioni 2013b, n.p.).[1] Literary works by Somali authors are published in multiple languages; Somalia did not have an official alphabet until 1972, when the Latin alphabet was introduced and recognized.[2] Shirin is a native Somali speaker, but as she moved to Italy before 1972, her written Italian is better than her written Somali. *Lontano da Mogadiscio* became a landmark text in Italian postcolonial and migration literature and was reprinted by Datanews three times, in 1994, 1997, and 1999. The novel's fourth edition, *Lontano da Mogadiscio / Far from Mogadishu*, was published in 2013 by Laurana in e-book format and in an expanded, revised, bilingual version (Italian and English, translated by the author). This edition offers new reflections on the Somali diaspora, on dislocation, on cultural identity, and on the search for a reconciliation between past and present.[3] These ideas also emerge through her participation in Asha Siad's short film *Memories of Mogadishu* (2018), which compiles the memories of those living in the city before the outbreak of the Civil War in 1991.

Shirin's second novel, *Nuvole sull'equatore. Gli italiani dimenticati* (2010) is set during the Italian trusteeship in Somalia. Key themes of the novel are the protagonist Amina's agency and her emancipation from male authority (Burns 2013, 57), and the discrimination experienced by her daughter Giulia because she is a *meticcia* person. The translation in English, *Clouds over the Equator: The Forgotten Italians* was published in 2017 (Shirin 2017a).

In 2017, the author's first collection of poems in English, *Wings*, was also published. The collection was subsequently published in Italian. One of these poems, "Mare Nostrum," inspired Elizabeth Bossero's composition for the flute "Silentium Nostrum" (2018). Shirin's second collection of poems, *I Suckled Sweetness*, was published in 2020, and her poems were also included in anthologies of contemporary Italian poetry (Shirin 2022a, 2022b).

Shirin's intellectual and public activity is not limited to her writing; it also encompasses her research and presentations at cultural institutes and universities (Brioni 2020, 18–19). For example, from 2013 to 2016 the author was on the advisory committee for Transnationalizing Modern Languages, a research project aiming not only at creating innovative methods for teaching modern languages and cultures in universities but also at developing research practices that could impact culture and society beyond academia.[4] Shirin's appointment recognizes the relevance of her creative work to postcolonial and decolonial studies in the Italian context. Shirin also conducted two creative writing workshops, "I Write with More Than One Voice" and "Writing across Languages and Cultures," that included writers from Nigeria, Sudan, Somalia, Croatia, France, Bulgaria, and Poland, who had immigrated to the United Kingdom. The workshop's composition mirrored the cultural and linguistic diversity in Birmingham. The project's website emphasizes that interdisciplinary activities facilitate "a better understanding and communication between and across diverse cultures," inviting workshop participants to examine the "role of translation, understood in its broadest sense, in the transmission, interpretation, and sharing of languages, values, beliefs, histories, and narratives." Moreover, these transnational and participative research practices offered new resources and theoretical tools to answer a key question in a globalized society: "How do people respond creatively to living in a bilingual or multilingual environment and to identifying themselves as mobile individuals or communities?"

## Islam and Me

Shirin developed the core of "Io e l'Islam" (*Islam and Me*) in 2007. The first draft, a poetic account of the discrimination Muslims experience in Italy, was completed in 2009. In 2018, Shirin rewrote it using the poetic draft as its impetus and source material. I edited the text in synergy with Shirin between 2018 and 2020. The text was originally published in Italian with the title *Scrivere di Islam. Raccontare la diaspora*. Shirin translated the original text in English between 2020 and 2022. In its current form, *Islam and Me* is an autobiographical account that develops into a critique of the media's erroneous connection between Islam and extremism.[5] At the same time, *Islam and Me* testifies to the undeniable impact this representation has on many Italian Muslims, who are subjected to verbal and physical abuse in a suffocating atmosphere of hostility and hatred. According to recent research, "Many Italians see . . . Muslims as a threat to national safety: four out of ten disagree with the claim that Islam is a peaceful religion" (Dixon et al. 2018, 104).

This perception of Muslims in Italy has greatly influenced the internal political debate. For instance, the xenophobic political party Lega Nord (The Northern League)—which has played a significant role in recent Italian history and has been part of four government coalitions (1994; 1999–2003; 2008–2011; 2018–2019)—tried to prevent Muslim communities from building mosques in Italy, a right that is granted by article 19 of the Italian Constitution. *Islam and Me*, as the title suggests, narrates the personal experiences of a European citizen who is considered to be "different" due to her skin color and the wearing of the hijab. Shirin recounts a story familiar to other Muslim women in Europe that counteracts a uniform and homogenizing account of Muslim culture.[6]

*Islam and Me* is divided into five chapters written by Shirin, one coauthored chapter and a coauthored coda. The personal dimension suggested by the title invites the reader to appreciate the ways in which individuals interact with collective identities, whether religious or national. The first chapter, "Dear Italy," recounts several episodes the writer experienced while she was living in Italy and shows the change in the social perception of African immigrants from the 1970s to the present. "Dear Italy" speaks of Shirin's ambivalent relationship with Italy, summarized in the last sentence of the section, "From the Locals' Perspective": "To look at Italy from within and from abroad is an exercise I could happily do without. This is my country, too."

The second chapter, "My Daily Islam," narrates her relationship to her faith and her daily spiritual practice. This chapter includes prayers and a subjective explanation of the precepts of Islam in daily practice. Shirin features other Muslim women's accounts, sometimes using the third person singular, sometimes the first person singular, as if to underscore her proximity to the stories she is telling. Although this section describes a personal spiritual journey, it is possible to read it in relation to other sections of the text where Shirin discusses Islamophobia and the inability of Italian institutions to respect religious freedom—a reading that sheds light on the political dimensions of private experiences: religion may offer shelter and protection from a society that is often hostile. Moreover, the account of Shirin's private religious experience has political implications because Muslims are often depicted as a collective subject rather than as a group of individuals who experience their spirituality in different ways. Muslims compose 2 percent of Italy's population today. They are mostly Sunni but come from different countries, including Morocco, Albania, Tunisia, Senegal, Egypt, Bangladesh, and Pakistan. It is perhaps because of this heterogeneity that Italian Muslims have not been able to reply cohesively to the attacks they have received to date.

The third chapter, "Birmingham," compares Shirin's life in the United Kingdom to her past experience living in Italy. In *Lontano da Mogadiscio*, Shirin rediscovered Somalia through Italy; in "Io e l'Islam," the author looks at Italy from the perspective of life in the United Kingdom. In this chapter, as well as in other parts of the text, the author uses the first person plural pronoun to refer to, in different contexts, either women, Birmingham residents, Italians, Somalis, or Muslims, exposing the author's fluid identity and a sense of belonging that is constantly renegotiated. The section "Small Heath Park" has a special role in the chapter as it describes the neighborhood in southeast Birmingham where the Ghamkol Sharif Mosque, one of the biggest mosques in the United Kingdom and a point of reference for Muslims and Somali people in Britain, is situated. The documentary *Africa Is You: The Somali-Dutch Community in Birmingham, UK* (2016), by Linde Luijnenburg, Ahmed Magare, Dennis Mulder, and Anna van Winden, was filmed in this neighborhood, which testifies to its centrality in the affective geography of Somali migrants in the Midlands.

In the fourth chapter, "Islamophobia," Shirin documents the accounts of many women and men who have been subjected to racism because they are Muslim. As Laura Mahalingappa, Terri Rodriguez, and Nihat Polat point out, religious discrimination has psychological, emotional, and social implications; thus it is important to safeguard any religious belief in its diversity (2017, 4–6). The stories that are gathered in this chapter remind us that for too long Catholicism has been presented as an invisible norm which traditionally defines the Italian identity.

The fifth chapter, "Contradictions," presents Shirin's critiques of the *umma*, the community of Muslim worshippers. Shirin's inability to connect with some interpretations of Islam's precepts inspired my relationship with the subject of this study. I am not a Muslim, and my interest in this religion is a way to promote not only religious diversity but also secularism in Italy. In a country where the word *cristiano* (Christian) is still used as a synonym for "person," to understand different religions is of primary importance to the protection of civil rights (Brook and Jansen 2022).[7]

One could see this book as stemming from the critical reflection Charles Burdett initiated in *Italy, Islam and the Islamic World: Representations and Reflections, from 9/11 to the Arab Uprisings* (2016), albeit from a different angle. Burdett advocates a reexamination of Italian studies, one that stresses the presence of new subjects and new identities as a result of migration. The most complete study of representations of Islam in Italy to date, *Italy, Islam and the Islamic World* analyzes various "cultural practices of signification" (Burdett 2016, 7), including novels on Muslim migrants in Italy, texts on the Arab Spring, travel books on Iran and Afghanistan, and sociological essays on Muslim communities in Italy. Burdett also focuses on journalist Oriana Fallaci's racist texts and conspiracy theories, which present Islam as intending to destroy the "Western world" (Fallaci 2001, 2004a, 2004b).[8]

In addition to the subject matter, Burdett's text inspired the creation of this book because it was written in a manner that attracts the general public, despite being targeted at an academic audience. Moreover, *Italy, Islam and the Islamic World* demonstrates that "though it may be tempting to think of Italian culture as in some way self-contained, separate and distinctive from other cultures . . . it is continually defined and redefined by its interactions with social and economic phenomena from across the globe" (2016, 15). By applying a transnational dimension to the study of a national culture, Burdett poses questions that are vital to understanding the postcolonial, multicultural, and multireligious identity of contemporary Italy: "What is the nature of the Italy that we study? What is the meaning of the nation state in a transnational world? How can we think beyond territorially bounded notions of Italian culture? Are our methodologies adequate to address a social, cultural, and *religious* reality that is, under the pressure of globalization, changing at an extremely rapid pace?" (2016, 198).

To address some of these questions, the sixth chapter, written by Shirin and myself, explores the collaborative process leading to the publication of the print editions and English translations of *Lontano da Mogadiscio / Far from Mogadishu* (2013) and *Clouds over the Equator* (2017a) / *Nuvole sull'equatore* (2017d). "A Dialogue on Memory, Perspective, Belonging, Language and the Cultural Market" is written in the form of a dialogue and discusses the opportunities for people belonging to minorities to express themselves. This conversation preceded our decision to write *Scrivere di Islam. Raccontare la diaspora* collaboratively, in a hybrid form, and through an open-access publication platform. If "minor" literature invites us to overcome the conceptual barriers of nation-states and to reconsider ideas of identity and alterity, literary criticism needs to follow this example and find new strategies for discussing the content, context, and experiences of authors. We believe that collaborative writing—intended both as a methodology and as a research trajectory—can be one of these strategies.

The hybrid dialogue between Shirin and myself focuses on the five main themes mentioned in the title. The chapter concludes that although literature written by authors who immigrated to Italy is still considered "minor," it has transformed Italian culture, introducing new questions and ways of communicating into the critical debate. In this sense, Shirin's career is representative of the experience of many authors who immigrated to Italy and attempted to contradict the dominant narrative about immigration—which casts it as a problem—despite an unwelcoming publishing environment. This collaborative text aims at providing suggestions for how the humanities can be conceptualized, including its relationship to a practical problem, namely the urgency of listening to the voices of immigrant artists and intellectuals in Italy. The coda is also a coauthored text which further discusses our collaboration and reflects upon the making and the initial reception of *Scrivere di Islam. Raccontare la diaspora*.

## Italian Postcolonial Literature and the Cultural Market

Chapter 6 is a development—and, partly, a translation—of the collaborative essay "*Lontano da Mogadiscio* and *Nuvole sull'equatore*: Memory, Perspectives, Belonging, Language, and the Cultural Market," which was commissioned for a forthcoming academic volume on "minority" cultures in Europe. Although Shirin's ideas are appealing to an academic audience, finding a general interest publisher for her work proved particularly difficult. Indeed, both *Far from Mogadishu* and *Clouds over the Equator* have been published via the Amazon self-publishing service CreateSpace. This paradox is a constant element of Shirin's publishing history: while her work has circulated in academic journals, edited volumes, and websites specializing in migration literature like *El Ghibli. Rivista di Letteratura della Migrazione* (El Ghibli. Journal of migration literature), she has often struggled to reach a general audience.

Our collaborative process leading to the publication of the English translations of *Lontano da Mogadiscio* and *Nuvole sull'equatore*, and to a subsequent new Italian edition, differed from the traditional relationship that exists between a writer and a literary critic. My contribution to the publication of *Lontano da Mogadiscio / Far from Mogadishu* was not limited to the writing of the introduction. I took charge of the editing and proofreading, communicating with the publishers and marketing the book. I had a very similar role in the publication of *Nuvole sull'equatore* and *Clouds over the Equator* in 2017. For *Scrivere di Islam. Raccontare la diaspora*, I wrote the preface and coauthored a text with Shirin. I was editor and curator of Shirin's "Io e l'Islam," where I suggested potential stylistic and formal amendments. My contribution to the text itself was limited to proposing bibliographical references and posing questions to Shirin. In return, Shirin offered suggestions on the introduction and reviewed the final version. Moreover, our dialogue was fundamental to the writing of my monograph, *The Somali Within*, from both a linguistic and a cultural standpoint.

Collaboration is not unusual in migration literature; indeed, it is constitutive of this specific literary production. Since the 1990s, Italian migration literature has featured innovative authorial models, which differed from those of "canonical" literature. Texts like Pap Khouma's *Io venditore di elefanti* (*I Was an Elephant Salesman: Adventures between Dakar, Paris, and Milan*) (1990, edited by Oreste Pivetta); Carla De Girolamo, Daniele Miccione, and Mohamed Bouchane's *Chiamatemi Alì* (Call me Alì) (1990); Mario Fortunato and Salah Methani's *Immigrato* (Immigrant) (1990); and Alessandro Micheletti and Saidou Moussa Ba's *La promessa di Hamadi* (Hamadi's promise) (1991) have involved extensive collaboration between multiple parties. Analyzing twelve collaborative works written between 1991 and 1997, Daniele Comberiati and Bieke Van Camp underscore how Italian coauthors took on various roles, including "coauthors . . . curators . . . or author[s] of the introduction . . . , maintaining an active role in the ideation and writing of the text" (2018, 93–94). Comberiati and Van Camp also highlight the influence of the Italian coauthor's profession in determining the type of text that was produced: "The works by a coauthor who is a journalist feature socioeconomic considerations, and the narrative plot functions to highlight this aspect; when the coauthor is a writer, the style remains similar to that of the Italian writer's previous and consecutive literary works; lastly, when the text is coauthored by an academic, footnotes and bibliography become fundamental elements" (2018, 93). As a result, these interactions have produced texts that are extremely difficult to categorize. For example, Comberiati and Van Camp show that *Io venditore di elefanti* not only is a literary work but also offers insight into the study of Italy's changing social reality (2018, 100).

Collaborative works addressed the "political urgency of telling stories concerning migrants' life and aspirations that are different from those recounted by . . . the media" (Burns 2007, 136).[9] At times these collaborations resulted in misappropriations and disagreements (Burns 2003; Parati 2005, 99–100). Often Italian coauthors were seen as responsible for the text's narrative style, while the migrant's or, more recently, the "second generation" writer's personal experience legitimized the story's authenticity.[10] As Comberiati and Van Camp demonstrate, this vision implies that the "foreign author" is presented as a "witness rather than a writer" and overlooks the fact that the migrant coauthors were intellectuals and writers in their own countries and "had intellectual profiles that could definitely manage the autonomous production of a text" (2018, 94).

These collaborations are inspired by oral communication, and therefore they focus on a dialogical dimension in which translation processes and intercultural communication strategies assume a fundamental role. In this sense, there is continuity between the collaborative experiences of the 1990s and more recent examples. I am thinking, for instance, of the narrative community that emerged in the documentaries I codirected with Graziano Chiscuzzu and Ermanno Guida, *La quarta via. Mogadiscio, Italia* (The fourth road: Mogadishu, Italy, 2012) and *Aulò. Roma postcoloniale* (Aulò: Postcolonial Rome, 2012) and that I cowrote with Kaha Mohamed Aden and Ribka Sibhatu, respectively. In the documentaries, Aden and Sibhatu tell the story of their native countries, Somalia and Eritrea, while at the same time retracing the legacy of Italian colonialism in the cities they live in, namely Pavia and Rome. *Aulò. Roma postcoloniale* and *La quarta via. Mogadiscio, Italia* are hybrid products, both autobiographical accounts and film essays, that reference historiography and cultural theory. They were made through collaboration with historians, translators, writers (including Shirin), literary critics, and musicians (Brioni 2013a). Eventually, *Aulò. Roma postcoloniale* and *La quarta via. Mogadiscio, Italia* were distributed with print volumes by an independent publisher and film producer in Rome: Kimerafilm.[11]

Another interesting example of participation and hybridization in cultural works addressing colonialism in Italy is *Timira. Romanzo Meticcio* (2012), by Wu Ming 2 (Giovanni Cattabriga) and Antar Mohamed. The adjective *meticcio* in the title not only refers to the collaboration between authors of different ethnicities but also describes the combination of texts, including primary sources, letters, and photographs. For this reason, *Timira* can be seen as either a creative nonfiction book or a fictional book based on historical sources and on Isabella Marincola's direct testimony. This mosaic of genres is a constitutive trait of the collective of writers in Wu Ming's cultural production. Indeed, their novels feature a list of the primary sources consulted, which include historical essays and often comment on the narrative techniques they utilize. Wu Ming 1's (Roberto Bui) "New Italian Epic 2.0" (2008) uses the essay form to problematize the dichotomy between criticism and artistic practice in contemporary literature. According to this text, theoretical reflection on the act of writing is constitutive of Italian literature from 1993 to 2008. This aspect is also present in *Timira*, which features four letters in which Wu Ming 2 interrogates his role in the collective writing process of the novel. In this sense, *Timira* successfully combines the linguistic experimentations of a writer belonging to one of the most successful writer collectives in Italy and the narrative methods of a "minor" literary genre such as migration literature. Indeed, *Timira* references some short stories and novels by Somali Italian authors, such as "Dismatria" (2005) by Igiaba Scego, in which Isabella calls Somalia her "matria" (mother country; Wu Ming 2 and Antar Mohamed 2012, 282), and *Nuvole sull'equatore* (Wu Ming 2 and Antar Mohamed 2012, 516). Reflections on collaboration, such as those appearing in *Timira*, do not feature in collaborative works of the early 1990s, and they demonstrate the coauthors' increasing awareness of and respect for the cultural influences that they are experiencing.

However, I believe that to see an evolution from coauthored texts inspired by the writer's biography to single-authored novels with seemingly more articulated narrative structures might overlook the fact that the first texts published by migrant authors in Italian have presented new authorial subjects, and experimental and collective forms of narration. In other words, to describe this process as an "evolution" might undermine the impact of literary works that not only displayed "new possibilities . . . for conceiving of human identity, but also suggest[ed] new ways of creating a text" (Bond 2018, 101). I do not want to underestimate the importance of migrant writers' self-representation, but the critical emphasis on single-authored models in migrant writing can be seen as a "normalization" of the authorial figure and the role that the "author" embodies in Western culture and in the commercial marketplace.

It is equally important to point out that the texts have undergone a creative process that has increased their reach and longevity. I already referred to the cases of *Lontano da Mogadiscio*, originally published in 1994, which became a bilingual text with additional reflections from Shirin about her migration to the United Kingdom in 2010, and of Ribka Sibhatu's *Aulò. Canto-Poesia dell'Eritrea* (Aulò. Song-poetry from Eritrea), a children's book published in 1993 that became a documentary in 2009 (Brioni 2014). One could also mention Fernanda Farìas De Albuquerque and Maurizio Jannelli's *Princesa. Dal Nordest a Rebibbia: Storia di una vita ai margini* (1994), a text that was transformed into an interactive project edited by Ugo Fracassa and Anna Proto Pisani in 2013. Another relevant example is the new Italian edition of Geneviève Makaping's *Traiettorie di sguardi. E se gli altri foste voi?* (Makaping 2022b), an autobiographically inspired text and anthropological reflection about racism in Italy that was originally published in 2001. Giovanna Bellesia Contuzzi and Victoria Offredi Poletto's English translation of the new edition of *Traiettorie di sguardi, Reversing the Gaze: What If the Other Were You?*, was published by Rutgers University Press in the same book collection as the present volume (Makaping 2022a). The book also inspired a documentary directed by Elia Moutamid: *Maka* (2023; Brioni 2022b). Far from being "fixed" in their original publication format, these texts went through processes of translation, adaptation, revisitation, and expansion, which were the result of collaborative efforts.

Hybridity is a main feature of this volume, and it characterizes Shirin's literary production since its very beginning. Many academic articles emphasize *Lontano da Mogadiscio*'s hybrid nature, given that this text is at the same time a travelogue, an autobiographically inspired story, an account of life in a city devastated by the Civil War, and a journalistic essay that has been introduced to the Italian audience by a journalist, Alessandra Atti di Sarro (1994, 8–10). For this reason, Rhiannon Noel Welch defines the narrative voice in *Lontano da Mogadiscio* as "autobiographical and anthropological" (2010, 217), and Burns claims that this text is "at once familiar (autobiography, testimony, narrative) and perplexing (all and none of these)" (2001, 177). Loredana Polezzi describes *Lontano da Mogadiscio* as "a patchwork of passages, often less than a page long, which take a multitude of forms: from the poem to the mini-historical essay to the etymological gloss, the anecdote, the list, or the intimate diary entry. [. . .] The fragmented structure of the [text] is also symptomatic of the fractured personal and collective histories with which [the author identifies]" (2006, 219). In other words, *Lontano da Mogadiscio*'s narrative form mirrors its subject matter, and its description of a diasporic experience cannot be reduced to a specific genre.[12]

After the publication of *Lontano da Mogadiscio*, Shirin gave several interviews to discuss the book and its main themes that were published in academic volumes.[13] These interviews suggest that research on the diaspora requires a dialogue between academics and immigrant writer to understand the narration of migration in all its complexity. These participative texts not only testify to academic interest in Shirin's work but also suggest their authors' intention to overcome the limits of a Eurocentric humanities education and to better understand the multicultural reality of contemporary Italy.

My collaboration with Shirin in *Scrivere di Islam. Raccontare la diaspora*, the book from which this English translation was developed, prompted me to question the role of cultural workers through my own personal experience, starting from the assumption that academia is not an impartial space of knowledge production. Rather, it is a context that needs to be constantly reinvented because it is troubled by social, economic, and historical tensions. As I wrote in a blog post with Cecilia Brioni on collaborative practices, there is still a tendency to view professors in the humanities as elitist, solitary figures whose approach to understanding modernity originates from their innate individual qualities and their studies rather than from their experiences in the world (Pease [1990] 1995). Collaboration helps to break the boundaries between disciplines, enriching textual analysis and above all situating research practices in a social and cultural context: "To show that knowledge originates from a dialogue locates the researchers' activity within a set of power relationships broader than just those expressed by the omniscient figure of the 'genius' or the one-way relationship between a single author and a 'text' to analyze" (Brioni and Brioni 2018).[14] The Italian literary canon is a clear example of the production of patriarchal, classist, white, Catholic, and heteronormative privilege: to call it into question means to rethink what defines Italianness and who is excluded from this "imagined community" and from the rights that belonging to it entails (Brioni 2015, 145–155). Migration literature completely changed my perception of what I considered "Italian literature" and suggested new questions and priorities for scholars working in the field of Italian studies. In my personal experience, it interrogated the ways in which my research practices either allow or contest the perpetuation of this privilege.

*Scrivere di Islam. Raccontare la diaspora* emerged from a dialogue between a scholar and a writer. Arguably, critical thinking and interpretation are fundamental to creative writing, but sometimes it is difficult for reflections developed outside academia to enter the scholarly debate. Likewise, creative writing offers a model for critical analysis developed in academia to reach broader audiences through a more accessible narrative style. This approachability can also facilitate civic education. In our current social and political context, finding new ways of conveying different perspectives which challenge a unilateral and Eurocentric vision seems particularly important especially when it comes to countering harmful and racist narrations about Muslims in Italy.

Our way to question a traditional model of knowledge production was to collaborate on the making of this volume, which is neither an academic essay nor an autobiographical account, although its revision process conforms to the academic textual production process where numerous professional figures (peer reviewers, editors, and copy editors, among others) collaborate on the creation of the literary work. The text also aims to problematize the idea that literary criticism can interpret a literary work better than the author can. This concept is reminiscent of a colonial model, especially when it refers to postcolonial or migration literature in Italian. Indeed, our collaboration went against the model of the white literary critic having the last word on the work of a writer of African origins.

Contemporary Italian culture cannot be limited to national borders. Its analysis requires a redefinition of disciplinary fields (Burdett and Polezzi 2020; Burns and Duncan 2022), which might create a welcoming cultural space that mirrors today's multicultural, multilingual, multireligious, and multiethnic Italian society. I believe it is fundamental to interrogate Italian studies' role in enabling the exclusion and ghettoization of foreign or minority subjects, in terms of gender, religion, race, and class. We need to develop a model that respects pluralism, intercultural translation, differences, and the complex transnational geographies that constitute every person's story. The issues surrounding the marketing and publication of *Lontano da Mogadiscio* and *Nuvole sull'equatore* inevitably had us facing questions about the uneven relationship between who controls the production of knowledge and who is subjected to it. This collaborative text is an answer to these considerations. To examine the practices through which knowledge is produced is not new to certain members of the academic community, especially those with an activist orientation (Gustavsen 2003). For example, the ideas behind the Decolonize the Media collective (Mirzoeff and Halberstam 2018, 123) and those stated in *Decolonising the University* (Bhambra, Gebrial, and Nisancioglu 2018) are similar to those we adopt in our project.

Traditionally, the humanities have long privileged individual achievements over collective efforts and prioritized theoretical research that had little connection to practical matters. Although a theoretical approach to culture might be useful to better appreciate practices aimed at social change, the urgency of discussing the discrimination of Muslims in Europe led Shirin and myself to develop a *meticcio*, a collaborative, hybrid text, that we hope will inspire new participative practices. If today the decolonization of Italian studies is a priority (Brioni, Orton, Parati, Zhang 2022), we wish for an increasing number of artists, activists, and researchers to put their talents and skills into practice to develop new forms of understanding between people of different cultures. These experiments would bring about methodological enrichment, the development of new theoretical standpoints, a better ethical and cultural awareness, and new attention to the questions expressed in migration literature so that academic research and public engagement can successfully contribute to the pursuit of social justice.

Simone Brioni
State University of New York at Stony Brook

# Note on Translation
# and Alphabetization

Somali, Eritrean, Ethiopian, and Arabic proper names are mentioned by referring to the first name, which is the most common practice in African studies. This choice has been taken to avoid the ambiguity caused by the Westernization of these names. For instance, Shirin Ramzanali Fazel is most frequently mentioned in scholarly literature as Fazel, but also as Ramzanali Fazel. However, both of these simplifications have no linguistic legitimacy, and they might create more problems than they solve.

All English translations of the Quran are taken from the website https://al-quran.info/.

Islam and Me

## ~ 1 ~

# Dear Italy

### The Official

I am at the Venice airport, having traveled back from England, where I live, to see my daughter Salima. The immigration official is in his thirties; he has a goatlike beard, thick glasses, and dark eyes like the black olives of the Mediterranean. He is scrutinizing my Italian passport. Then, overcome by curiosity, he asks me, "*Signora*, how long have you been an Italian citizen?" Encouraged by his young, smiling face, I reply, "From back when Italian TV shows were still in black-and-white." In my heart, I'm thinking, "Long before you were born. Is my nationality printed on my brown skin or my hijab?"

## Reciprocity

I am an Italian of Somali-Pakistani origin. I am Muslim. Unfortunately, I don't feel represented by those newspapers, politicians, and TV programs that depict us with stereotypes: *immigrati*, *terroristi*, *criminali*, people coming to Europe to steal jobs, bringing disease. I feel rejected, insulted, censored. I hear people say, "Italians are Italian by blood; immigrants can't become Italian." What an insult!

I do not deny my origins, my culture, my religion. I bring them with me; I am proud of them, and I live them daily. I am the result of many life experiences, many encounters, all of which have enriched my identity. I have changed so much in my life that I am still able to reshape my way of thinking, if necessary. I feel good in my skin. That's who I am.

I grew up in Mogadishu during the 1960s. We all knew each other in the neighborhood. The doors of the houses were open; we had uncles and aunts who took care of us, even if they were not blood relatives. We played in the alleys, and we felt protected. My childhood was happy. I grew up in an independent Somalia. Independence was celebrated, and there was great enthusiasm toward building the country after decades of Italian colonial rule.

At that time, I had no idea that the African countries' borders had been determined by the colonial powers and their interests, and the Europeans, the colonizers, had indoctrinated us in their language and their culture. We had been taught a history that was solely from their point of view.

I didn't go to Italy; it was Italy that first came to me. It had come into my hometown of Mogadishu, and I was crossed by that border. The streets, schools, churches, military barracks, monuments, shops, movie theaters, restaurants, bars, and hotels had Italian names. Even after independence Radio Mogadishu still broadcast news, songs, and daily programs from Italy. The Milan, Inter, and Juventus football teams had their fans. The national newspaper, *Il Corriere della Somalia*, was printed in Italian. Italian was still the country's official language until 1973, when the Somali language became the official language, written with the Latin alphabet.

My family wanted to give me the best education possible, so I went to kindergarten and elementary school at the Regina Elena Institute run by the sisters of the Consolata Missionary Order. This school followed the same curriculum as those in Italy and was recognized by the Italian Ministry of Education. It was primarily for Italians living in Mogadishu, but it also enrolled a limited number of children from the local elite including children of the Somali and foreign bourgeoisie and foreign government officials.

My parents were both Muslim, but I never heard them speak badly of the nuns or of Christians in general. Somalia is a predominantly Muslim country. Nonetheless the capital is home to the Cathedral of Mogadishu, which was built and inaugurated in 1928, the same year my mother was born. The cathedral is in the Norman Gothic style and was copied from the Cathedral of Cefalù in Sicily. This was not the only place of worship for Christians in Somalia; Mogadishu also had the Church of the Sacred Heart as well as important cities, such as Merca, Brava, Chisimaio, and Baidoa, where Catholic places of worship could also be found.

At my school, there was a room for prayer, complete with an altar, a tabernacle, and candles. There we knelt on the cold marble floor, the smell of frangipani in the air. In the garden, there was a statue of the Virgin Mary holding the Baby Jesus. At Christmas the nativity scene was set up, and the performances were prepared. In the morning, before starting the lesson, we had to stand up, make the sign of the cross, and recite the Hail Mary.

I remember how frightened I was by the nun's face as she stared down at me through her glasses and said accusingly, "Whoever isn't baptized goes to hell!" I was not baptized. The image of the devil—half man and half beast with horns and a long tail, scornfully pushing sinners into the flames of hell with a pitchfork—terrified me. I'd never had the courage to talk about baptism at home. Sitting at the family table having lunch, I would watch my mom and dad as they ate—they weren't baptized either. With each bite, I swallowed my doubts and fears.

As a child I received a great deal of conflicting information. Catholics argue that those who are not baptized carry the original sin, but the Quran maintains that Muslims do not carry original sin. I did not know what the Trinity was, but I knew my Catholic friends believed in it. I needed time to process the whole matter. Fortunately, my daily life intertwined with Islam, a religion that is also a way of life. I did the five daily prayers and fasted during the month of Ramadan. My parents taught me that Islam is *wanaag uu samee deriskaga*—above all, doing good for others. I watched my mother helping those in need as best as she could. She would take groceries and well-kept clothes to the widow and her children who lived just a few steps away from us, comfort the family that had lost a child, prepare lunch for the children whose mother was in the hospital, and give to the poor person who knocked at the door begging for a hot meal or a few coins. During the Eid festivity and in the month of Ramadan we also shared our food. We visited our sick neighbors. We prayed and attended the funerals of people we were not very close to. During the wedding ceremonies women cooked, danced, and sang together. New babies were showered with gifts. There was a strong sense of community, and this helped me to develop an empathic attitude toward others.

Today, unfortunately, I live in a world where Islam is demonized and hostility toward Islam has become the norm. Newspapers in Italy defame and attack Muslims as if they were a monolithic mass, undifferentiated; they equate them all to a small group of terrorists. "Bastardi Islamici" was the main headline in *Libero*, a major national newspaper, after the November 2015 Paris attacks. On the pretext of free speech, the media foments hatred of Islam and legitimizes violence. Physical and verbal attacks against migrants, asylum seekers, refugees, and Muslim Italian citizens have increased. Muslims are forced to pray in garages and basements, not to mention on sidewalks; they are often even denied the right to open a mosque. Terrorism kills Muslims every day, but in the eyes of many, these lives do not count—they believe that all Muslims are terrorists.

Politicians and journalists discuss Islam without having any specific background in it or having done research. They associate the term *jihad* exclusively with terrorism against the West. *Jihad*, for a Muslim, is the daily struggle and inner spiritual striving to live as a Muslim. *Sharia*—a code for living that Muslims should adhere to, which recommends praying, fasting, and donating to the poor, and which regulates inheritance rights and marriage and divorce—is largely presented as signifying stoning, cutting off hands, and beheading. I ask for nothing more than my rights as an Italian Muslim citizen to be respected. I ask for a little reciprocity.

## Labels

Have we become commercial products? It was no longer enough that we turned into billboards displaying the various brands affixed to our clothing and accessories. Today, even our complex identities are labeled.

When I read, "the Muslim journalist," "the Muslim mayor," and so on, I find it simplistic and racist. Think about whether someone should write, "the Christian journalist," "the Christian mayor."

Then I wonder: "Which Islam do people refer to as this religion is so diverse?"

The European Islam?

The Italian Islam?

The jihadist Islam?

The secular Islam?

The cultural Islam?

The moderate Islam?

The political Islam?

The radical Islam?

The reformist Islam?

The Salafi Islam?

The Shiite Islam?

The Sufi Islam?

The Sunni Islam?

The Wahhabi Islam?

I get lost in these divisions. The Latin motto *divide et impera*, divide and conquer, echoes in my mind.

Religion has become a label or, worse still, a color. But religion cannot be given a color. As there are Arab and African Christians, white and Black, there are also American, French, English, German, and Italian Muslims, white and Black. Religions are universal. The media paints Muslims of a single color, without understanding that they are talking about very different people.

## The Gladiators

I'm watching Italian television and inevitably the people on it are talking about Islam, or rather Islamists. It is one of those televised debates that, whatever the channel, tries to attract the largest possible viewership. The speakers, the tone, the words used, however, are always very similar. There are a host and a panel of guests including the "expert" who raises his voice to shut down the others if he does not agree with their opinion. It's a screaming match, a format aimed at valorizing fearmongers and Islamophobes. The TV guest keeps repeating, "Muslims must adopt the values of the Western world." But how can they judge what Islamic values are if they don't know Islam? Islam is built on universal human values such as the sacredness of life and property, equality, justice, and peace. Is intolerance a fundamental value in Western culture? Of course, I know not all Westerners—whatever this label means—would agree with that.

Occasionally the format shifts to feature a confrontation between two antagonists: one a Muslim and the other an ex-Muslim who has become a fierce enemy of Islam. My living room is suddenly transformed. I am at the Colosseum, catapulted as if by magic into ancient Rome at the time of the gladiators. I hear the crowd incited by words, which have the power to wound more than swords. The so-called ex-Muslim is in the armor of an "expert." He violently hurls phrases taken from the Quran at his opponent. It is incredible how one can make a book say anything by quoting one of its passages out of context. The anger is contagious, and it spreads through the audience. The guest is screaming, "Islam is a violent religion! Women are subjugated by men who force them to wear the burqa. Their men kill them if they don't comply with Islamic laws." The opponent is trying to explain, his rival is shouting, their voices overlap, the audience applauds.

In the general cacophony meaning is lost, but it doesn't matter: the Muslim guest has been denigrated; his body will be dragged from the arena during the commercials that precede the next TV program. The studio audience enjoys seeing stereotypes about Muslims reinforced—stereotypes created by their own deeply held, deeply rooted prejudices.

But I'm also a fighter, and I'm not discouraged by these gladiators.


## The "Interview" with the Muslim

It doesn't matter if the victims also include Muslims; after a terrorist attack in Europe, it's always the same scene. An ambitious woman journalist, lurking outside a mosque, rushes up to a group of worshippers, usually after Friday prayers. Many of them are young Moroccans, Tunisians, Bangladeshis, Pakistanis, and Senegalese. They speak a simple Italian they have learned from television or from colleagues. They are not illiterate; they have studied and speak English and/or French as well as Urdu and/or Arabic and a dialect. They have adapted, taking on physically demanding low-status jobs while putting their dreams and expectations aside in order to support their families at home. The microphone is thrust into the faces of these young men, and they are asked direct and insolent questions: "What do you think about the Christians they killed in the church?" or "Do you feel like justifying those responsible for this attack?" or, even worse, "From a religious point of view, do you share the views which led to this attack?" Many are unprepared for this unexpected verbal violence and don't know what to answer.

Others have not even understood the question. Still others, frightened, don't even stop to hear the journalist's questions and are taken for hypocrites or are presented as people who support the terrorists, because, by implication, "those who keep silent are complicit." Sometimes it happens that some brave boy does stop and tries to answer. He tries, with difficulty and fervor, to express his thoughts. He is not used to speaking in front of cameras; he is visibly in trouble. I observe this scene and feel a sense of disgust about the way the interview is being conducted. I instinctively think, "It's like stealing candy from a child!"

In the second version the scenario changes. This time the interview is conducted inside the mosque after congregational prayers. Some worshippers have arrived late and are immersed in the ritual of praying privately. The journalist wears a transparent scarf from which a lot of her hair protrudes. "Well, fancy that!" I think and wonder, "Is it perhaps television sleight-of-hand trickery, meant to delude the potential Muslim viewers about the 'freedom that is enjoyed in the West'?" It's no coincidence that the journalist is always a woman: perhaps the message they want to convey is that women are discriminated against by Islam. The journalist is about to interview the imam on duty. I write "on duty" because in Islam prayer can be led by any Muslim who knows how to recite the Quran. For example, if a group of friends are at home or in the park and the time has come to pray, it will be up to the most learned among them to lead the prayers. His role is temporary, unlike the role of a Catholic priest. During the interview we see the poor imam fighting back courageously, trying to explain very delicate and complex concepts in a language that he has not yet mastered. His courage deserves praise, but the damage the media causes is enormous.

Can Muslims really speak out in today's Italy? Or are these interviews no more than monologues already scripted in which the interviewee is only an "extra," playing a bit part?

In Islam, as opposed to Catholicism that has the pope as its spokesman, there is no ecclesiastical hierarchy. Unfortunately, this makes for a lack of cohesion; because of this and many bureaucratic obstacles, it is hard to organize some means of confronting and countering the embarrassing accusations spread by the media.

## The Boy from Via Gluck

Adriano Celentano's "Il ragazzo della via Gluck" is one of my favorite songs; it reminds me of my own story. Although it was released in 1966, it is still very popular in Italy. I recently discovered that there is a beautiful version in English, "Tar and Cement," which Verdelle Smith recorded that same year.

Celentano's autobiographically inspired song talks about a boy who lives on Via Gluck, a street in Milan's rural outskirts. He is forced to move to the city center with his family and is sad to leave the place where he was born. His friends envy him because he will have more opportunities and comforts in the city, and he will no longer have to wash outside in the yard. The boy tells them that they are the lucky ones because they can continue to play barefoot in the meadows, while he will be "breathing concrete." Eight years pass, and the boy finally returns to Via Gluck. He was forced to move because his family was poor, but now he has money. However, his money cannot buy back his childhood or reclaim the land now covered in asphalt and concrete.

Although "Il ragazzo della via Gluck" takes place in Milan, it tells the story of many people from the South of Italy who left their homes to go to the North in search of work when massive industrialization was profoundly changing the country. The fatigue and painful separation from one's homeland are reflected in these lyrics. It's a nostalgic song, a reminder of how we can lose what we love the most. Every time I listen to it, it makes me sad because it takes me back to the early 1970s, when my husband and I first arrived in Novara, Italy, with our two-month-old baby. For political reasons, we too had had to leave my city, Mogadishu, which was radically changing after the military revolution. In Italy, this new country, we had no family nearby, no safety net. We had only ourselves to rely on.

My friends in Mogadishu didn't understand my sadness. I say Mogadishu, but among us we called the city by its affectionate name, Xamar. They thought I was lucky—I would be living in Italy where everything was at hand: well-stocked department stores, museums, movie theaters. They envied my freedom.

In Novara I discovered homesickness and isolation; we were the first nonwhite family to settle there. By contrast Mogadishu had been a multicultural, multiethnic city, and we had known each other a bit. We, the kids from the neighborhood, had grown up together, played together. When I left Mogadishu, I left my family behind and my own little world, which had given me a sense of security.

Everything around me was foreign in Novara, even the Italian I knew so well sounded different—like a dialect. There were so many elderly people on the streets, walking dogs on leashes. I dreamed of being able to open the window one morning to see my blue sky or walking barefoot on Lido beach, of seeing familiar faces around me, hearing the sound of the *af somali* in the *suuqa* markets.

The Civil War in 1991 destroyed so many things in Mogadishu, and I am well aware that I won't find my home again or the friends of my teenage years, who are gone. The Arch of Umberto I by the park where I played as a child, the movie theaters where my parents and I used to go, both have turned into rubble.

While Celentano talks about the urbanization of Milan and how the world he knew has changed, I think of the devastation of Mogadishu during the war: houses shattered by bullets, women raped in front of husbands, brothers, children, fathers, telephone lines cut isolating the country from the rest of the world, bandits looting, families dispersed, no food, no running water, and no electricity.

I have a painful feeling and wonder: Why brother against brother? Why destroy our city, our heritage? Why don't they let my city shine, full of children who want to laugh and play, barefoot and free in its ancient dusty streets?

My Xamar no longer exists; it survives only in our memories, and that's why I insist on telling you about it.

## Babbo Natale

The controversy over Christmas emerges every year, inevitably, in Italian schools. Some school principals do not want to stage the nativity scene, and right-wing politicians and newspapers attack the school administration, accusing them of disrespecting Italy's Catholic traditions. The joy of this festive event is marred by the use of political language. Hatred is expressed toward the Muslim community, which is certainly not responsible for the dispute. Unfortunately, it happens that in our country, Christmas, instead of inspiring dialogue and a peaceful atmosphere, has created a campaign of terror in the media.

Commercially Christmas has crossed borders all over the world. I have seen trees decorated with Coca-Cola cans and coral on remote island beaches in Indonesia. In the shopping malls of Kuala Lumpur, long lines of parents wait to take photos of their children with Santa Claus, his reindeer, sleigh, and fake snow. A small, inflatable version of Santa Claus peeps out of some shop windows in Tunis or Hammamet. Yet these are all in Muslim countries.

For me Christmas brings back distant memories from the early 1970s when my family and I first arrived in Italy. In Novara we were the only ones to have brown skin. Everyone looked at us. People stopped us just to touch my daughter. It was very annoying. I remember back then that I wanted very much to blend in with those around me. In my heart, I didn't feel any different. Years of Italian school, films, novels, music, and food had contributed to my multifaceted identity.

Unconsciously I wanted to prove to everyone else that I was just like them. Over time, to my new friends, the greengrocer, the hairdresser, the kindergarten teacher, the ice cream maker, the people I met in the park, in a pizzeria or a cafe, sipping a cappuccino, I was no longer the Other. I was part of their community. Our brown complexions gave an exotic touch of color to the gray monotony that surrounded us.

In Mogadishu, for my family and me, Christmas was *panettone* time—that was when we had the traditional Christmas cake. It arrived in a cardboard box from Italy, and I couldn't wait to get up in the morning to eat this dome-shaped cake for breakfast, super soft, rich in raisins and candied oranges, which melted in my mouth. Its citrus, vanilla, and butter scent were unforgettable.

In Novara time passed and my own little girls started kindergarten. With Christmas approaching, together with the festive atmosphere and the little plays the children were in, Santa Claus—called Babbo Natale in Italy—arrived too, bringing presents for good children. We didn't want our daughters to feel as if they were different from their classmates—or worse, to feel they were naughty—so we decided to get our first tree.

An icy cold and light mist enveloped the city. In the street market the stallholders rubbed their hands to warm them, their cheeks were red and their eyes watery from the cold. There were stalls selling sweets, figurines for the Nativity scene, and Christmas decorations beneath the beautiful dome of San Gaudenzio. The smell of roasted chestnuts made our mouths water. The air was scented with Christmas trees; they were just the right height to fit in a small car like ours. All around us, smiling children were looking up at the magical trees.

It was getting dark and snowflakes were falling from the sky. The sound of the clock striking the hour signaled that Christmas Eve was approaching. In the crowd we were caught up in the frenzy. We had to hurry; we had to make our two girls happy tonight. Babbo Natale, the big cheerful man with the thick white beard, would be bringing gifts to our house.

Back at home, their little hands helped adorn the tree with gold, red, and silver baubles, green bells, and romantic little stars. Swathes of gold and silver garlanded the young branches. We laughed and had great fun. It was night, and we turned on the colored lights, which flashed intermittently. But they weren't the only lights in the room. You could also see the enraptured, shining eyes of our little ones. They looked like two kittens hiding in the dark.

## From the Locals' Perspective

In 2010, I moved to England where I took an active part in the cultural life of Birmingham, a vibrant and cosmopolitan city. I traveled and still travel around the world, but I'm not the typical tourist who goes to the beach, sunbathes, and takes a couple of photos. I spend a lot of time talking to local people, I read the English editions of local newspapers, I like to explore different neighborhoods. The way people look at me on the train and on the bus, the attitude of shop assistants toward me teach me more about the world I live in. In short, I try to look at the cities I visit through the eyes of those who live there. This kind of approach to the other, to the new, to the different, is also the way in which I see my own country, Italy. I observe how this Italy of mine has changed in almost half a century; there are now four generations of my family with Italian roots.

Year by year I follow what's happening in Italy through online newspapers, satellite TV, blogs, books written by academics and journalists, and the accounts of Italian friends with whom I remain in touch. I go back to Italy, where I have my home, at least twice a year. I could easily turn my back on what is happening politically in Italy—in other words, *fregarmene*—but I can't. Why? I have asked myself this several times, and the answer is because I feel Italian. I love the country in which I spent my adult life, where I raised my children and buried my parents, and where my grandchildren are now growing up. For this reason, I get very upset when I read or hear such false and misleading statements about immigration or Islam. I feel entitled to point my finger and raise my voice.

When I am back in Italy I go to the mosque, and I often hear the children there speaking Italian. They laugh, play, and talk about sports and football stars. If I close my eyes and only listened to their voices, I wouldn't be able to distinguish them from other Italian children. They were born in Italy; their parents come from Morocco, Senegal,

Pakistan, and Bangladesh. I see veiled girls shopping, chatting among themselves in Italian, like many of their generation. They feel Italian, but by law they are foreigners. In Italy the right of citizenship is acquired through *jus sanguinis*, the right of blood: one of the parents must be Italian, no matter where their child was born. If not, these young men and women, who were born in Italy, cannot participate in a school trip outside the country. They cannot be exchange students abroad. They cannot apply for school grants. They are now petitioning that Italy's citizenship laws be reformed and *jus soli*, the right of birth and naturalization, be adopted.

This proposal is opposed by some politicians. Have the champions of *jus sanguinis* ever tried to put themselves in the place of these young people born and raised in Italy? Have they ever tried to imagine what these people feel when they are rejected and insulted, when they realize that in the country where they were born and which they consider their own, their opinions and their words count for nothing? Has anyone ever tried to imagine what an Italian girl in a veil feels when the school principal decides to ban headscarves because her choice can be interpreted as a provocation and arouse contempt and ostracism from her schoolmates? Who protects her when she walks the streets of her city?

When children are brought up to get to know and respect those different from them, a society is created, which is—I won't say "tolerant," because it's a term I don't like—but open and multicultural. When I look through the eyes of those who want me to exist in their image and likeness, I don't recognize myself. I don't even recognize my country through their eyes. To look at Italy from within and from abroad is an exercise I could happily do without. This is my country, too.

# Residence Permit

In Italy, it is the beginning of autumn, the days are still sunny and mild. It is 2006, and I can't wait to become a grandmother for the second time. That morning my daughter called me. "Mom, it's time to go to the hospital, I'm going into labor." "We'll come at once," I reassured her.

At the time we lived within walking distance of each other. My husband and I rush to her house. It's her first baby—I'm more agitated than she is—and my son-in-law is away in Germany on business. After about half an hour's drive, we arrive at the hospital in Bassano. Every time we stopped at a red light, it seemed endless.

At the hospital, the nurse asks her for her documents. Samira hands over her national health card and her identity card. The woman looks them over and says, "Signora, have you *permesso di soggiorno*?" Taken by surprise, my daughter says, wide-eyed, "Why would I need a residency permit? I'm Italian." The nurse, without lifting her eyes from the forms, stutters an apology. My daughter and I look at each other. I am undecided whether to laugh or to make a scene, but my daughter is appalled. It is the first time she has ever been asked if she has a residency permit. That question was like an abrupt kick, more forceful than the straining within her. It numbed her for a few seconds. It was as if even the baby wrestling in her womb had heard it and gone still.

Samira was born in Italy, to Italian parents. She graduated in Padua. Italy is her country. The question was completely absurd and hurtful to her, but perhaps it was also a sudden awakening; it caused her to understand that to many, she is not seen as Italian.

The day my grandson Jibril was born is a joyful memory, but it also reminds us of that episode. We had another surprise that day, too. The midwives, relatives, and friends expected to see a newborn baby like those in a Benetton advertisement—one with curly hair and a *caffellatte* complexion. Instead, a curly blond-haired boy was born, with very fair skin—not at all *caffellatte* but *latte*, the color of milk.

## Marocchino

In Italy the term "Marocchino" no longer refers, as it did until recently, simply to an inhabitant of Morocco or to a particular kind of coffee but has become a derogatory term to indicate any brown-skinned person. Being a "Marocchino" can mean being an illegal immigrant, a rapist, a thief, a criminal, or a drug dealer. Sometimes this expression is used hypocritically with a hint of patronage in the small town in Veneto where we live. I wonder how children from Morocco who grow up in Italy feel about that?

I would suggest to people who use this term in a derogatory sense to take a trip to Morocco. I did it with my grandchildren. Bilal was six years old and Nahila eight. The journey to Morocco changed our lives and enriched us. I had no idea what the kids expected, but I know that we still talk about it, years after. We left our hearts there.

The beauty of Morocco is indescribable, the Atlantic with its sparkling waves, the colors of the markets, the *medina*, the *souks*. We were not staying in a hotel but through our butcher, who sells halal meat in Italy, we managed to rent an apartment in Tiznit in southern Morocco.

Tiznit is a small, clean, friendly town famous for its silver jewelry. The walls of the medina date back to 1882. Its souks are alive, teeming with life, with colors, with joy, and with perfumes; they elicit all five senses. There are mountains of oranges, figs, spices, dates. There is music.

Our friend's extended family welcomed us as if we had been relatives. They opened the doors of their homes to us. We had lunch together, sitting around a table scooping chicken, lamb, and vegetable tajines from the typical cone-shaped terracotta dishes. We relished the bread, which smelled of anise and cumin. Their children played with my grandchildren during our monthlong vacation. We went to the beach; we visited the oases in the desert.

To go to Aglou beach, we took a taxi or a bus. We traveled along a stretch of deserted road, saw flocks of sheep merging with the landscape and small clusters of new white houses adorned with bright spots of bougainvillea. Watching the passengers, some dressed in traditional clothes, getting on and off the vehicle was a sight. The ticket was purchased directly on the bus from a girl in uniform, very pretty and always smiling. Aglou is fully equipped, has a clean beach with small restaurants where they serve tasty fish and couscous dishes. Not far from the beach there is an ancient stone mosque. When it's scorching hot outside, inside it's cool. The walls are painted white, and in some places the limewash is peeling off because of the salt in the air. The shadows and the silence bring peace to the soul and encourage recollection. The wool rugs are hand-knotted, and their Berber designs are perfectly in tune with the environment.

In the evening with our new friends Latifa, Malika, Rashida, Ziad, Zubeir, and Muhammad, we chatted on benches under streetlamps breathing the fresh air scented by the jasmine bushes, sipping mint tea served by a street vendor while the children played happily, chasing each other beneath a starry sky.

My grandchildren have a caramel complexion, and when they return to Italy from summer holiday, they become chocolate brown, especially the boy. Back at school, in the playground, an older boy called my grandson "Marocchino." Bilal, in a confident, ringing voice and a Venetian accent, replied: "I'm Italian, but I've been to Morocco and it's beautiful!"

## Holidays in Tunisia

It's mid-June and many Tunisian families who live in Italy travel on Tunisair. As the plane rolls up the runway for take-off, you can hear the children counting backward "dieci, nove, otto. . . ." Once in flight, I feel so moved when I hear a little girl's voice shout enthusiastically: "Le sfumature delle nuvole!" (Just a hint of cloud!).

What a joy, that trip—only a couple of hours from Venice, surrounded by color: the blue of the armchairs, the white ceiling, and the sea-blue carpet, almost as if anticipating the beach that awaits us. By the sea, the children scream in Italian as they dive into the waves. Italian is their language and under the beach umbrellas I recognize many faces already seen in previous years. We have a chance to chat to them— people from Bologna, Nuoro, Rome, and Turin. There are also several Italian Tunisian couples.

It's a sunny day. The sea sleeps in the sunshine, blue as the eyes of a newborn baby. White clouds seem to play notes of jazz music. I walk toward the bay, my feet bathed by gentle waves. I gather small solitary shells that have been hidden under the wet sand: they are shaped like biscuits. My thoughts are ruffled by the sea breeze. I feel a tickling in my shoulder: it's the sun before it becomes pitilessly hot. I reach the Sinbad Hotel. White beach umbrellas are lined up where a small group of elderly tourists are recharging their aching bones with the energy of the regenerating sun, hoping it can protect them from the next cold winter.

A strong, muscular young man, wearing huge dark glasses, walks by. He has a serious expression on his face and is holding a walkie-talkie. His big, shaved head turns slowly, like a radar antenna. He is scanning the beach with his eyes, trying to capture every movement. On his white shirt I read "Sécurité." The beach stretches for miles. I look at the immense sea. The sound of hooves catches my attention. Two armed policemen, riding bright horses with black coats, greet and overtake me. All around me it's divine until the music of the waves is interrupted by a quad bike that speeds along the shoreline. There are two policemen on it, armed with machine guns.

In this part of the Mediterranean, the summer season has not recovered since June 25, 2016, when thirty-eight people died in a terrorist attack. Yet nature has not changed. The sun still rises at the same time. The sea is salty and transparent, and the seagulls dive lazily.

The Italian Foreign Ministry announced, "It is not safe to travel to 'certain' countries, including Tunisia." However, there are many Italians who, like us, are here on holiday. Despite the efforts of the local authorities and the huge amounts of money they pay out of their meager budgets to guarantee safety to their guests, tourism languishes. The population suffers. Young people are unemployed and many, in pursuit of hope, are taking to the sea.

## Hijab

I would like to tell you about an episode that happened to me about ten years ago. I'm in the pediatrician's waiting room. I accompanied my daughter who brought the baby for a check-up. There were other mothers with their babies. A young lady sitting next to me kindly asked me: "Why do you cover your head?" This is the kind of question I like, leading to dialogue. I was about to respond when another lady sitting in front of us intervened and stated: "If they don't wear it, they are killed."

Even today these words sound to me as piercing as a drill in the ears, yet many years have passed since that day.

For a moment I was speechless and, in my mind, immediately began to scroll through the images shown on television: a woman covered by her blue burka while being stoned. I have bitterly noticed how much confusion is created in the minds of people who do not know Islam and how our memory has the capacity to store wrong concepts, which are then difficult to eradicate. Naturally I replied that mine was a free choice and that nobody would have killed me if I had not worn the veil. I also pointed out that my daughter, sitting next to me, did not wear it and was alive and well.

Many times, we have so little time to respond to sudden verbal aggression. I noticed that over the years the same question, "Why are you wearing the veil?" is asked of all the women who wear it when they are interviewed on television. The answer is always the same, "It's my free choice. . . ." And yet, the interviewer must always point out, "You do, but how many other girls are forced by the family to wear it?"

Enough! We can't take it anymore. . . . The veil issue has become a real obsession. There are a thousand reasons why a person decides to wear it:

For tradition.
Because it's fashionable.
To define one's identity.
By compulsion.
By ideological or religious choice.
And I can go on forever.

I wear the hijab for devotion, and I must add that in my family it was never mentioned. In Mogadishu, the hijab was the last of our thoughts. My mother, like all Somali women, wore the traditional *garbasaar*, a light veil covering her head and shoulders. I felt so much joy in finding old schoolmates who cover their heads. We shared the memories of our adolescence and rediscovered the complicity of when we were young girls.

During my travels in the world, I lived in Saudi Arabia for several years with my family and I was never forced to wear a veil as a foreigner.

Mine has been a long spiritual journey. It is not easy to explain what that little fabric expresses when I put it on. When I started wearing it, I also received criticism from some of my friends who considered me an "emancipated" woman. I made a conscious decision because I know both the West and the East well, and I am sorry to hear those who comment on my choices without knowing anything about Islam. How do these people understand what a woman feels when she serenely lives her spirituality and is comfortable with herself? How do they understand the experience of a woman who today wears the veil, her courage, and her determination? To wear the veil means to ignore looks of contempt, to see job interviews refused, to be teased with ignorant jokes. But is it better to be forced not to wear it for fear of being attacked or marginalized?

I ask my Italian sisters: try for once to imagine yourself on the other side. Don't judge another woman just because she has a piece of cloth on her head.

I recently heard a journalist label the customs of Islam as retrograde. Retrograde in comparison to whom and what? But above all, how much insecurity does it show about those who want to label them? Imagine if I had to ask every woman

I meet: Why did you get a dragon tattooed on your leg? Why did you pierce your tongue? Why did you dye your hair green? Why are you wearing ripped jeans? Why are you wearing boots? Why are you topless? Why did you shave your hair? Why do you, nun, cover your head? I would surely be taken for someone who doesn't mind her business, right? So why do others allow themselves to judge or would like to ban what I want to wear?

IT'S MY BUSINESS!!!

## Harem

I no longer remember which museum I was in while looking at paintings from the late nineteenth century. I pause to look at a painting depicting a woman covered by transparent kaftan showing her voluptuous breasts. She wears flashy jewelry. She is lying languidly on the sofa. It looks a lot like Eugène Delacroix's painting *Odalisque* (1825). It is a scene from the East, a product of pornographic European imagery. None of these painters has ever been able to set foot in the rooms, separate from the rest of the house, in which Arab women live. The harem is not a place of pleasure, yet it is depicted as if it were a brothel for noble or wealthy men. I thought, "Here is another insult dishonoring the Muslim woman."

## Burned Alive!

One of my first pleasant memories of coming to Italy was discovering the secondhand book stalls near the fountain of Piazza dell'Esedra in Rome.

In Mogadishu the only libraries that existed were in the cultural centers of the various embassies. The Italian Cultural Circle also had books available, but they were the classics of Italian literature: the works of Dante Alighieri, Ludovico Ariosto, Giosuè Carducci, Ugo Foscolo, Giacomo Leopardi, Alessandro Manzoni, Giovanni Pascoli, Giuseppe Ungaretti, and Luigi Pirandello, which we were already studying at school. The Gialli Mondadori, the Urania or Liala romance novels were sold in the stationery shop. To read something different in Italian you had to rely on exchanging books with classmates.

In the book stalls of Rome, I discovered the voices of other Italian and foreign writers. For example, I searched for the work of African writers, even though they were often confined to the narrowest stall. It was here I found Italian translations of extraordinary books originally written in English or French, such as Doris Lessing's *The Grass Is Singing* (1950), Frantz Fanon's *The Wretched of the Earth* (1961), or the poems of Léopold Sédar Senghor.

Over the years, my passion for books has led me to discover that many of the lessons I was given at school were incomplete and misleading. For example, as a young student I had always imagined the poet Pascoli as someone with a gentle and sensitive disposition, only to find out later that he proved himself to be a convinced nationalist in his speech "La grande proletaria si è mossa" (The great proletarian, she has risen!) (1911), intended to justify the Italian intervention and expansion in Libya.

In the bookshops of my own city, Vicenza, in the early 1990s, I saw the birth of a new type of literature, usually autobiographically inspired. Books such as Zana Muhsen's *Sold!* (1992), Souad's *Burned Alive* (2003), and Mende Nazer's *Slave* (2002) very much emphasized the image of Islam as violent and hostile to women. I do not doubt that, as in all societies, Muslim women, too, suffer violence and abuse. However, generalizations and stereotypes are often reinforced by this type of literature. Over the years, stories of this kind seem to have quadrupled. These "biographies" are weapons of mass distraction, instruments created for the dissemination of a distorted image of Islam in the collective imagination of Italian readers.

## Muhammad and the Quran

It's the beginning of a new school year (2017–2018). There's a wind of change blowing in our house. We are very excited; my granddaughter is starting middle school. Nahila knows that this is a very important step for her. The teacher who was with her for the five years of elementary school will no longer be part of her life, but my granddaughter will always remember her. On her last day of primary school, classmates exchanged kisses and hugs, and inevitably some furtive tears were shed. We're thinking about the future and life goes on. There will be new teachers and new classmates for Nahila in the second stage of her education.

One afternoon, my granddaughter and my daughter come to see me on their way back from the stationer's. After a very long delay, the new textbooks have finally arrived. Nahila is very excited. We sit on the sofa and start glancing through them. We have high expectations. In the history book, *Incontra la storia: Fatti e personaggi del Medioevo* (Meeting history: Events and people in the Middle Ages) by Vittoria Calvani, there is a chapter on the Arabs. As we leaf through the pages, the chapter title, "*Maometto* and the New Religion," catches our eye. My granddaughter is intrigued and asks me, "Grandma, who is *Maometto*?"

I honestly never expected to read that name—a distortion of the Prophet's name—in the new millennium. It was like a cold shower. Today kids use computers and are very curious. Before I can utter a word, Nahila types "Muhammad" into the search engine and finds a biography of Prophet Muhammad (peace and blessings to him). In this way she discovered that in the Middle Ages he was considered a heretic and a criminal, so the name *Maometto* was born from the union of two words, *Mal* and *commetto*—a derogatory term, coined to express contempt for the Prophet. I read on, and to my great dismay in this book I find many inaccuracies about Islam and the Arabs. I am patient and begin to correct it. There's a chapter in which a Bedouin talks about himself and says that "our ideal is to wage war and to carry out raids," as if the Bedouins were brigands (Calvani 2017, 82). Then it says, "my mother, one of the many wives of my father, wears the *chador*," as if the *chador*, which is worn by women in Iran, were worn by women in the Arabian Peninsula.

*Arab* in Semitic means "nomad." The same people are also called *badu* "man of the desert," which in Italian we translate as "Bedouin." However, the term "Bedouin" is given a negative meaning in this text, highlighting the raids and wars involving the glorious Bedouin tribe. This negative meaning is used to justify the image of a violent temperament, which has been attributed to Islam. In reality, the text is contradictory because on the one hand it says that Arabia is inhabited by Bedouins, and on the other it denies the presence of humans in the territory saying that "Arabia is a land of deserts and oases" (Calvani 2017, 84).

Apparently, according to Calvani, the Quran is a sort of copy, a collection of characters and prophets from the Judeo-Christian religions (Calvani 2017, 86). It even goes so far as to say that "*Maometto* had strong connections with Jews and admired their monotheistic religion, which contrasted with the disorder of Arab polytheism" (Calvani 2017, 87), forgetting, however, that Muslims have always said that Islam is the continuation of a single original message, at the heart of which are two main concepts: the uniqueness of God and the importance of submission (in Arabic, *islam*) to Him.

Several paragraphs are devoted to Prophet Muhammad, but his real name is mentioned only in passing; then the book continues to use the derogatory name *Maometto* (Calvani 2017, 87). It says that "in 610 *Maometto* had the vision he had long been waiting for" (87), while in reality the Prophet did not expect the archangel and was frightened when Gabriel appeared in front of him. Then it says, "The archangel Gabriel gave him the Qur'an, the book destined to become the sacred text of the Arabs" (87), thus making it seem as if the archangel had given the Prophet a book fresh from the press, while according to tradition it took twenty-three years of revelations before it was complete so that believers had time to assimilate it, memorize it, and implement its teachings. But most importantly, the Quran was revealed for all humanity and not only for the Arabs.

An image of the Prophet is then presented, specifying that Islamic laws were soon to forbid any representation of him—without telling us the source of this information. A caption specifies only that "*Maometto* wins over the poor but is forced to take flight from Mecca—the hegira" (Calvani 2017, 87). But the worst paragraph comes when it mentions holy war. Calvani writes,

> In Medina the persecuted Prophet became a religious, political and military leader. His preaching changed tone. It was no longer just a question of returning to social

equality; the new goal was Islam, that is the "submission" of all Bedouin tribes to the one God, Allah, and the end of polytheism. [Muhammad] sent his followers to attack the Arab caravans heading for the holy city. The booty served to feed those who were faithful to Allah, while Mecca became impoverished and its prestige decreased, *Maometto* called this offensive *jihad*, "holy war," and its success demonstrated his remarkable military qualities. In 630 Mecca was conquered by force of arms, the images of the gods were destroyed and the entire population of the holy city paraded before the Prophet swearing faith in Islam. With his "submissive" Muslims—that is the meaning of the word *Muslim*—*Maometto* then set out to conquer all of Arabia. When, two years later, in 632, the Prophet died, the jumble of tribes divided among themselves had become an *umma*, a community of believers ready to express their new energies in the name of a great goal: the conquest of boundless territories in the name of Allah, in obedience to the message of war launched by the Prophet. (2017, 88)

This passage does not explain that the freedom to choose one's faith is a fundamental Islamic principle, that the Prophet entered Mecca humbly, did not put his enemies to the sword, and did not deprive the losers of their possessions. Later there is discussion of Islamic laws and the condition of women, stating, "Women did not enjoy freedom of movement; they could not have responsibility in the civil and religious field (only today are we starting to discuss whether a woman can be an imam); [and] they could not decide their own destiny (for example to choose the groom) or that of their children" (99). These statements are misleading because they refer to a "cultural" Islam and do not take into consideration what women's rights were before the advent of Islam. Islam gives women the right to education, to express their opinion both in religious (there have been women *ulema*—Islamic scholars—including Aisha, the wife of the Prophet) and in legal or financial matters. A woman has a recognized right to inherit, to possess her own assets, and to conduct economic activities. In Islamic marriage it is a mandatory condition that the woman freely gives her consent to that marriage in the presence of witnesses. In case of abuse or incompatibility with her husband, she has the right to request a divorce.

I tried to find information about the author online, but the few articles I was able to track down talk about the impossibility of finding information on Vittoria Calvani. We only know that "she has published 32 books with Mondadori," even if she is not "a historian by profession" and is not "affiliated with any university" (Clericetti 2016). In particular, an article by Carlo Clericetti criticizes Calvani, accusing her of offering a distorted image of Italian history as well.

Our society has changed, and therefore I think it would be appropriate, in the case of a school textbook discussing Islam, to set up a commission composed of Muslim academics to examine the texts before they are published in order to avoid prejudice and misinformation in the minds of the young. The creation of an active multicultural society— serene, cohesive, and respectful of the dignity of everyone regardless of gender, ethnicity, or religious belief—begins precisely with these young people who are growing up side by side in school.

## Islamic Lessons in School

In San Felice sul Panaro, in the province of Modena, the school board of the primary school in via Montalcini has decided to further enrich the cultural baggage of young people with Sunday classes on Arabic and Islamic culture. The lessons take place from 9:00 A.M. to 12:30 P.M., are open to about two hundred children from six to fourteen years of age and are organized by a voluntary association.

Controversy broke out immediately and ended up in parliament where ministers were questioned by center-right deputies, and there were even threats of legal action. This uproar convinced the head of the school to change his mind even though the initiative had been agreed upon by the school board.

A few days later, to be precise on January 14, 2019, I read an article in the *Corriere di Bologna* titled, "Sunday school lessons on Islam: the head teacher suspends classes." Immediately after reading this and thinking about it, I said to myself, "Another lost opportunity for Italy!" and thought, "Isn't it better to hold Sunday lessons on Islam sanctioned by the authorities?"

I am convinced that one of the fundamental requirements for true integration is to know about one's own culture and other people's too. I think that denying one's origins or not being able to learn the language spoken correctly by one's parents creates cultural gaps and enslavement. For this reason, it is essential that the "hour of religion" at school should not be an hour of catechism, but rather a way of learning more about religions.

On our journey through life, it is our experiences and our intellectual curiosity that shape our identity as individuals. We are the ones who choose who we are and what we want to be. Only societies reluctant to change—or those that want to hold on to certain privileges unaltered—try to define, within themselves, fictitious social hierarchies based on stereotypes and preestablished labels.

Episodes of this kind make me sad. These walls, these barriers, this totally negative attitude toward the different, which makes any dialogue impossible, are harbingers of future calamities and serious wounds in the fabric of society. This is not what I wish for the country I love.

## Invasion and Escape

The "invasion" of Muslims. The "invasion" of immigrants. The word "invasion" reminds me of an enemy entering and occupying a territory by military force. It creates anxiety, and fear; I feel threatened in my home. Then I try to rationalize my fears, and I see an image of people pressed together in boats, of people with eyes begging for a little humanity: young people, men and women with their children who chose to risk their lives by traveling in those rubber inflatables across the sea. They are aware that there is a risk of dying overwhelmed by the waves, of perishing because they have no food and water, of not making it through suffocation, heat, or cold, but they choose to risk death rather than stay in a country where they are denied any social growth opportunities. I wonder, therefore, what kind of invasion is it? It is not a video game or online betting, where one is seated comfortably in an armchair, pressing buttons. They are not shooting a Hollywood movie. No victorious armies are entering the country in tanks, they are not bombing our cities with missiles or flocks of fighter bombers, they are not stationing mighty warships off our shores. They don't come to colonize our peninsula—far from it. They are real people with their fears and fragilities. They are mothers who hold their children to their breasts, pregnant women who do not know if they will ever see the child they carry in their womb. They are terrified. The only weapon they carry is called hope.

# ~ 2 ~

# My Daily Islam

## The Prophet

*We sent you only as a mercy for creation.*
—Quran (21:107)

This passage of the surah "The Prophets" refers to the Prophet Muhammad, who is the role model for every Muslim. The Prophet's life story is told step by step in the *Seerah* (his biography). Reading this text strengthened my faith because it is only when we have a deep knowledge of someone's life that we can love him without reservation.

When I was a child I listened to stories and anecdotes about the Prophet's life. Over the years I have continued to read and deepen my knowledge of his life from various authoritative sources such as *The Sealed Nectar* by Safi-ur-Rahman al-Mubarakpuri. I have learned to know every detail about him in his varied roles: as an orphan child, a husband, a father, a messenger persecuted for his beliefs and exiled, and as a political leader.

Sometimes I have heard the word "Mohammedans" applied to us Muslims. It's a mistake. For us, Muhammad is not God, but the messenger of Allah. He is a man with all his weaknesses, fears, and emotions. They are also the small gestures of his daily life that led me to love him. I see Muhammad as a husband who helps with housework or who mends his own clothes.

The *Hadith*, which uses an image from everyday life, describes Muhammad with his grandchildren in his arms and climbing on his shoulders. Or tells us how, when the prophet's daughter, Fatima, went to see him, he rose to greet her and made her sit in his place. I see the humanity of the Prophet in his love for animals, when he got up at night to go out into the cold if he heard a cat meowing; or when he personally took care of his camel, his donkey, or his horse. Muhammad always said we should not ride tired animals, make them carry loads that are too heavy, or treat them with cruelty. And he also said a worker should be paid before his sweat dries on his forehead—a principle that I find important to follow to counter the precariousness of life in the working world today.

I wept when the limits of decency were exceeded and a cartoonist caricatured Prophet Muhammad. I did not feel hatred, but rather I felt great sadness and pitied those who, cloaked in their ignorance, defend themselves by saying that this is the true face of the West—of its freedom of thought, freedom of expression, and freedom of the press.

I believe that these much-vaunted freedoms should not be separated from respect for others. This is what my daily Islam has taught me; this is the teaching of Prophet Muhammad.

## Jihad—Struggle

I start my day by practicing my *jihad*:

I cleanse my heart. I pray *Fajr*, the morning *salat*, and I thank my Creator for the life He gave me.

I am committed to being an understanding wife, a loving mother, a wise grandmother, a sincere friend, an honest person, and a better citizen.

I respect my neighbors and the elderly. I help the needy and try to spend my time fruitfully.

The words of our beloved Prophet Muhammad come to mind. When a poor man asked him, "I have nothing, what can I give to charity?" the Prophet replied, "Smile. To smile at a stranger is *sadaqa*—charity!"

Today I read in the newspapers that a "jihadist" is a terrorist, indissolubly associating terrorism (hateful actions carried out by a few villains who are exploited) with Islam as a whole. Brothers and sisters in Islam, brothers and sisters in humanity, let us repossess the word *jihad* by restoring its original, honorable, pure meaning: the effort made to achieve a goal and to satisfy God. For this, let us practice *jihad* together. Let us join forces and sweep away hatred. Let us, in our daily life, see that justice is done. Let us create a better world for our sons and daughters.

## Alhamdullilah

*Alhamdullilah*, thank you Lord.

For the everyday blessings I take for granted.

For the early morning rays of the sun that radiate into a Wedgwood blue sky.

My foot sinks into the sand as gentle waves caress the shore. The shore is deserted, and I swim in the safe crystal-clear waters like a newborn in his mother's womb. I feel it all belongs to me: hungry seagulls swooping down on prey, clumps of algae that float aimlessly, and the ocean that is whispering to me tales about pirates and mermaids.

*Alhamdullilah*, thank you Lord.

I am blessed every day with Your creation.

I was blind. I was numb and took everything for granted.

The sky is peppered with playful clouds that look like horses that gallop waving their long silky tails. My soul and my thoughts float. I can't hold back tears of joy.

*Alhamdullilah*, thank you Lord.

Allah guide me toward Your Light

## Allahu Akbar

The muezzin's call to prayer—*Allahu Akbar*, God is greater of all things—brings peace to my heart and tears of gratitude toward Him. A call that brings vivid memories of my childhood.

I remember as the dawn began to breathe. The neighborhood was still asleep, and I snuggled under the crumpled bedsheets. The strong melodious voice of the muezzin sailed from the nearby mosque to reach the intimacy of my room. I felt protected.

Five times a day, with devotion, I am standing piously on my prayer mat. I firmly declare: *Allahu Akbar*. Humbly I kneel, placing my forehead on the floor.

The day my little baby girl took her first wobbly steps I was so happy that *Allahu Akbar* escaped from my lips.

The first time I held my grandson in my arms and hugged this bundle of blessing. I could not hold back from exclaiming: *Allahu Akbar*. My heart was filled with joy.

At my father's funeral I was shrouded in sorrow: *Allahu Akbar*. He gave me the strength to accept that loss.

I watch the sky, the moon, the stars, the sun, His perfect creation, and my tongue sings: *Allahu Akbar*.

On the morning of Eid day, when I walk briskly toward the mosque, with every step I take I recite joyfully: *Allahu Akbar*.

At Hajj—my pilgrimage to Mecca—among crowds of pilgrims I supplicate: *Allahu Akbar*.

Why today is this phrase associated with terror and fear? To say that Allah is greater than all things perhaps sounds like a threat?

Allah is *Al-Muhyyi*—The Giver of Life—and wants us to preserve life.

He and only He is *Al-Mumit*, the bringer of death, and it is to Him that we will all have to answer on the Day of Judgment even if we have caused harm by perjuring His name.

## Life

With all its moments of joy and bitterness, life is a blessing, an emotional journey that takes me from the highest peaks of the mountains to the depths of the oceans.

I believe in my faith. Like everyone I waver and fall. In those moments I try to seize the rope of *Al-Muqtadir*, the Almighty, to support me.

Like a tortoise dragging its house, I carry with me the memories of the houses in which I have lived and all the sensations they have given me. I carry within me the words of my mother, my father, and the people who have been dear to me.

I travel with my suitcase full of dreams, those I have made and those I would like to come true. I look back and look around and realize that Allah has given me more than I expected. *Alhamdullilah*, I am blessed.

## A New Beginning

Every day is a new beginning for me. I open my eyes and rejoice in being alive. I am aware of the luck that I have been granted to be able to start again, and of the opportunity that I have been offered to reflect on my mistakes and to try to be a better person than I was the day before.

However, not all beginnings were joyful. When my father passed away suddenly and when my mother died after a long illness, I had to start all over again, and it was traumatic. Suddenly I realized that I no longer had their comfort, that I could no longer enjoy their presence, their wisdom and their stubbornness—so typical of elderly people. I felt lost. I missed them terribly, every moment of the day.

I could see the shadow of my father sitting in the kitchen and reading the newspaper while he sipped a cup of tea that smelled of cinnamon and cloves. At other times I seemed to see the figure of my mother in her flowered headscarf playing cards with my daughters. I missed hugging my father's broad shoulders. I missed cuddling my mother's tiny body in my arms. Until then, I had taken life for granted. The loss of my parents was my first encounter with death. Realizing so abruptly that life doesn't last forever made me think.

With the passage of time, I unfortunately forgot the lesson. I thought that everything revolved around me like the sun and the moon. Over the years, life has given me sadness, pain, and sorrow. Gradually I began to see the world with different eyes. I sensed that there was much more than my eyes could see. I began my long journey of introspection, searching for a higher purpose in this earthly life. I was longing for that true joy that fills the heart and soul. Who could fill my heart? Only the One who created it.

So now I find peace in every new beginning. When I submit to my Creator, the One who gives me life, He grants me, without judging me but with compassion, love and forgiveness, the ability to start again.

## The Power of Prayer

I have discovered the sweetness of the call to prayer, the inner voice that reminds me, "Stop, think, and reflect. Give yourself a break."

Other confused voices in my mind whisper to me instead, "Wait, finish reading this chapter, clean the kitchen, make a phone call, send a message on WhatsApp, reply to emails." Time is my worst enemy; unstoppable, every second that I am alive and breathing, it passes quickly.

Through prayer, I have discovered *Al-Rahman*'s kindness—*Al-Rahman* (the Merciful) the only one who reads my heart, the only one who listens to my wishes, and the only one who knows my problems, my joys, and my weaknesses.

I free my body and mind, submitting humbly as I rest my forehead on the floor. I feel immense peace. I know that *Al-Rahman* is watching me and that He is the most generous.

## A Moment's Pause

I am on vacation in Kuala Lumpur, surrounded by large architectural structures made of concrete and steel. They show the power of men. The majestic Petronas Towers defy the angry howl of the wind. Huge shopping malls grow like the wombs of pregnant women. A crowd of people, young and old, browse among major designer clothing shops, restaurants, cinemas, and jewelry stores. Materialism wants us to believe that we will be in this world forever. I am at Suria KLCC, one of the largest and most modern shopping malls in the world.

The time has come for *salat*—prayer. I head for the first *surau*, the prayer room.

I am in a room with ivory painted walls adorned with Arabic script. A soft blue carpet with delicate arabesque designs covers the floor. In one corner, on a birchwood shelf, there is a display of books on Islam and the Quran in Arabic, English, and Malay. Silence envelops me, immersing me in the serenity of this place.

The room gradually fills with women, most of them very young and beautiful creatures. Gracefully they take two pieces of fabric from the hangers, a long one-size skirt and a shawl to cover the head and shoulders. They wear them to cover tight jeans and the latest fashion in T-shirts.

A moment's pause in the chain of illusions and false paradise. Whispers of Allah's words fill the heart. They restore peace. The mind and the body abandon themselves. My forehead rests on the floor. I ask for forgiveness. I ask for strength. We are weak human beings. We ask Allah to guide us. His promise is firm in our hearts.

## Stolen Identities

Every act of terror and every news report of such events makes me feel helpless. It's as if my identity has been stolen, my religion stripped of its original content.

Because of the actions of criminals, Muslim men and women are, every day, being verbally abused and spat on. In our Western cities, we are viewed with suspicion. Our children are scrutinized in schools. Sometimes we are ordered to get off the plane because the passenger next to us feels threatened while we are reading the Quran.

Some countries deny us entry visas because we are labeled "terrorists." Our only fault is that we were born in the wrong country, have the wrong name, speak the wrong language, have the wrong complexion. Meanwhile, hate crimes are on the rise, but there is no room for such news on television news programs. Images of a pig's head are posted on the doors of our mosques, and our places of worship are set on fire.

I kneel before the Almighty and I submit to Him: may peace flourish in the heart of humanity.

## Modest Fashion

It's a beautiful spring day and I'm going shopping. New lines are on show in the dress department of a big store. I like light and fresh fabrics in cheerful colors that recall the summer. I'm looking for a modest dress. Unfortunately, I have no chance of finding it; the skirts are microscopic or have vertiginous slits, while the tops are excessively pinafore—exposing the arms. To wear these clothes, I have to try to combine them. For example, with the top I have to find a shirt with long sleeves to put over it or a pair of trousers to wear under a skirt with slits. I have to do this mental exercise before I buy to see if these combinations work. I wish department stores had a modest clothing section. I don't just want to wear black *abayas*. We Muslim women don't have to wear any particular clothes or a specific color. The important thing is that the dress is not transparent, not too close to the body, and arms and legs must be covered.

Famous fashion designers show their collections of luxury clothes for the Middle East on the catwalks of Dubai and Paris. It is a very profitable market; there was talk of an expected turnover of $484 billion in 2019. Yet on March 30, 2016, I read in the *Guardian* that the eighty-five-year-old Pierre Bergé, Yves Saint Laurent's right-hand man, addressed other designers asking them to "give up money and have principles" while at the same time defining Islamic fashion as "abominable" (Agence France Presse 2016). He accused the designers who helped to create Islamic fashion of taking part in the enslavement of women, and he continued his speech by saying that the task of designers is to make women even more beautiful, to give them the freedom to reject abominable garments that hide their bodies.

I have great respect for other people's opinions. What I want to emphasize is that the parameters by which we measure ourselves are, unfortunately, always Eurocentric. And then I don't agree that to be free a woman must only be beautiful and adhere to a canon of beauty often created by men. Today women don't really have the freedom to have a few extra pounds or a few more wrinkles. So what freedom are we talking about? I would like every woman to have the freedom to be respected, to be heard, and to be able to express her opinion without the fear of being judged or blackmailed.

Fashion houses like Dolce & Gabbana are welcome to include the so-called "Islamic fashion" in their collections. Actually, I don't think there should be an Islamic fashion, but rather clothes that can be worn by all women. What I hope is that in our everyday life, we Muslim women will be accepted for our own sakes, as individuals, and not for how we dress. If we decide to dress following the canons of modest fashion, we don't want to be stigmatized for this.

It does not irritate me that Western designers make huge profits on "Islamic fashion" or—you decide what to call it—"modest fashion." What bothers me is that, even if a woman could afford a particularly fancy and stylish veil, she would still be seen by the airport security officer as a criminal. I am European and Muslim, and I would like to feel included in this society, which is also mine. I just wish I could have the freedom to wear what I want without being discriminated against.

## Halal

Today it is so easy to put the stamp "halal" on meat products and restaurant menus. It has become a narrow concept, the slaughtering of an animal.

The word "halal" carries deep meaning. It needs introspection in our daily life. We have to ask ourselves: "Am I fair to my employees? Has the animal we eat been treated humanely? Am I cheating my customers?"

## Sharia

I asked my friend Lisa, "What comes to your mind when you hear the word *sharia*?"

She told me, "Women covered from head to toe, men marrying four wives, chopping hands and stoning."

"Is that all you know about *sharia*?"

Astonished she widened her eyes and added, "Is that not enough?"

"What do you know about *riba*?"

"Is *riba* the name of a god?"

"*Riba* applies to Islamic financial law. In Islam it is forbidden to apply interest on loans."

"What do you mean?" she asked, "I can borrow money with zero interest? Is it really forbidden by *sharia* law to charge interest on loans?"

"Yes," I replied.

Her jaw dropped: "It means the mortgage on my house will not double its original price?"

"No," I answered.

"That is marvelous! How come nobody talks about it?"

"If *sharia* law were applied in the world, nations would not sink in debts; there would be greater social equity and the risk of poverty would be reduced. This prospect is a threat to the capitalist system and large financial groups."

In a soft voice Lisa replied, "I wish we had this *sharia*, but it sounds like utopia!"

I don't understand how *sharia* law has become the symbol of the inability of Muslims to integrate into European society. *Sharia* law is a set of laws that contemplate many aspects of daily life that in the West are regulated by several legal codes. Yet the two systems legal matters are not incompatible, since we Muslims must first of all follow and respect the laws of the country in which we live.

## Islamic Countries

In the Western media I often hear the expression "Islamic countries." I travel in search of these "Islamic countries," but I only see dictatorial regimes, corruption, and oppression. Yet one of the names of Allah is *Al-Adl*, the One who brings absolute justice.

I have the impression that in the Western mindset a so-called "Islamic country" must be a country with a thousand restrictions. To me, there is no Islamic country that reflects the negative benchmarks created by the West. Traveling to countries where the majority of the population professes the Muslim faith, I have seen discos, cinemas, satellite dishes, and bars selling alcohol—and women who drive, work, appear on television, and dress in Western-style clothes. I hear young people mixing their language with English or French. So I would like someone to explain to me what the expression "Islamic country" means. Having said that, I believe that Islam and Muslims in general have accepted a cultural blend. On the contrary, it seems to me that the West is struggling to see beyond the stereotype "Islamic countries" of kebabs and couscous.

## Ramadan

In the holy month of Ramadan, I have been asked several times, "Don't you drink even a drop of water?" I am not asked, "Why are you fasting?" or: "What is the purpose of your fast?" The questions are focused on food and when we will be free to eat. To justify this custom we try to give answers in step with modern times and some praise the benefits of this practice, given that certain doctors say that fasting helps cell-regeneration.

For me the answer is much simpler: "I fast because it is Allah's command and I submit to His will. Fasting reminds me constantly of His presence."

Ramadan is the month when the first verses of the Quran were revealed. It is the month when I recharge my spirit by reflecting and deepening my reading of the verses of the sacred book. It is the month when I try to improve myself in my daily life by getting rid of bad habits. It is an opportunity to reconnect with humanity by forgiving and asking for forgiveness.

In the last ten days of Ramadan, *Leilatul Qadr* is the holiest night, the night of forgiveness. It is the night that is worth more than a thousand months, the night in which the angels descend to earth. Then I pray, imploring God, "Oh Allah! You are the One who forgives, You are the One who loves to forgive: Forgive me!"

## Mother's Day

On Mother's Day, supermarkets and shops compete with each other for the best offers on boxes of chocolates, flowers, perfumes, creams, and greeting cards.

I think of those mothers who wait all day for their children to knock on their door with a bouquet of roses, a box of chocolates, or just a hug and a smile—and, on the other hand, of those for whom the knock never comes.

I am also thinking of mothers who have lost a child or those mothers forgotten in nursing homes for the elderly, or those women who, even though they desired it, have never enjoyed the gift of motherhood.

During my childhood, Mother's Day and many other consumer festivals were not celebrated. For us, every day was Mother's Day. In fact, we have always been taught that "Heaven is under the feet of mothers." This statement has its origin in the story of a man named Jahimah who went to the Prophet Muhammad and said to him, "O Messenger of Allah, I want to go out into combat (*jihad*) and I have come to ask you for advice." The Prophet asked him, "Have you a mother?" Jahimah replied, "Yes." The Prophet responded by commanding him, "Stay with her, for Heaven is under her feet."

My mother always said to me, "Nothing belongs to us in this world. We came from nothing, we will leave with nothing, not even our children belong to us."

Allah has entrusted us with His gifts. We are His trustees, and we must take good care of the environment instead of destroying it. This is perhaps the most important lesson my mother taught me.

## The Angel of Death

We belong to Allah, and to Him do we … return.
—Quran (2:156)

The angel of death does not knock on doors, he takes orders from Allah. When our time is up, we have to leave. Without warning, without any date, without a minute more or less, life is taken from us. The doors of earthly life close behind us; our loved ones, our possessions, our career, everything that had importance in this world is taken away from us.

Death is a summons to all of us, a deadline that humans forget easily. We cling morbidly to life, and society leads us not to accept the idea of getting old. We fall in love with earthly things—money, success, riches, love, and power— and we want to have more and more. At the call of the Angel of Death, everything suddenly disappears, like a mirage in the desert. We find ourselves alone and unprepared.

Allah, make me one of those who do not forget about Your mercy. You are the Generous, the Compassionate, the Loving.

## Traveling

I love traveling. I am fortunate to live in this technological age when I can easily move from one continent to another. I love meeting people, discovering new cultures, exchanging ideas, borrowing recipes, and learning new languages. Traveling, I feel that I am honoring my Islamic duty.

I am grateful to Allah for giving me and my family the opportunity to be able to live in various countries. I am aware that, by deciding to live and work abroad, we have made a great gift to our daughters, giving them the opportunity to meet people of different cultures and to have the privilege of having formed their own identity as citizens of the world.

Unfortunately, nowadays everything is done quickly with the excuse of having little time. Trips organized in groups with guides are alienating for me. They show you the artistic and architectural jewels of a city at supersonic speed. There is no time and no way to exchange a few words with people. And the above verse of the Quran invites us to do the exact opposite.

Meeting other people is important. My last intercontinental trip took me to Malaysia, a melting pot of different peoples and languages. In Kuala Lumpur, distances are enormous, and in my taxi journeys I have conversed with people of all ages—male and female, Muslim, Hindu, Christian and Buddhist—all Malaysians. Listening to their stories allowed me to better understand the dynamics existing between the various social groups. Despite having traveled a lot, I feel I will never ever finish discovering the world.

## ~ 3 ~

# Birmingham

### I Am a Brummie

I have traveled,
visited many countries,
heard various languages
met faces of different colors
but I have never found so much human diversity
as in this place.

In every park and behind every door
voices and people from all over the world manifest
    themselves.

They arrived before me
from distant countries, from the former British colonies

India, Pakistan, Jamaica and Hong Kong
to work hard in textile industries.

After years of struggle against
fanaticism and racism,
today they own property,
invest in society,
they have become teachers and lawyers,
journalists, actors and professors,
doctors and Members of Parliament.

Since I have lived in this city,
I have noticed whole run-down neighborhoods,
renewed and made lively
by new restaurants, bakeries, and shops
owned by Somalis, Afghans, Turks, and Iraqis.

They bring pride and hope to their communities
win gold medals at the Olympics
waving the flag of the United Kingdom.

I walk through the streets
observing the past and the present;
Victorian homes, new residential areas,
and then temples, churches, mosques, and *mandir.*
Buildings so different to my eyes—
they carry only one message
of love.

Brummie by choice
I fight with my voice
fears and intolerance:

I share stories, poems and emotions
with other Brummies
who think like me
in this city that has so many stories to tell
just like me.

## Belonging

I feel at home in the city of Birmingham. It's a feeling I felt
from day one. There are no curious looks; everyone dresses
as they want and can come from anywhere in the world.

It is normal to be served by a salesgirl who wears a hijab.
It is normal to go to the hospital and meet a nurse with a
    hijab.
It is normal to find a teacher wearing hijab.
It is normal for a policewoman to wear hijab.
It is normal for girls to wear hijab to school.
It is normal to see a journalist on television in a hijab.
It is normal to get on a bus driven by a woman with a hijab.
It is normal to be visited by a doctor with a hijab.

It is normal to meet two married mothers at school who
    come to collect their child.
It is normal to be seen or operated on by a doctor with
    black skin.
It is normal to see a couple of boys or girls holding
    hands.
It is normal to see mixed-race couples with their beautiful
    children.
It is normal to see girls at school wearing *burkini* while
    swimming.

It is normal to see a woman driving in a *nikab*.
It is normal to see a policeman wearing a turban.

Normality is created when there are no divisions or labels.
Normality is created when a person is judged for his/her
professionalism.
Normality is created when a person is accepted for what
he/she is.

Italy is also my home despite the comments of people who want to force me to identify with one culture. For too many Italians, it seems almost inevitable or a duty for a Muslim who is born, grows up, and lives in Italy to forget, hide, or even abjure his religion and throw away his culture.

In England, the religious festivals of all faiths—Diwali, Vaisakhi, Eid, Passover, Christmas, Easter, and others are recognized and respected. It is this widespread sense of inclusion that makes me feel at home.

Every individual should feel accepted in the country in which they have chosen to live, work, grow, and educate their children.

## Speaking Italian

When I arrived in Birmingham in 2010, I did not often hear people speaking Italian around me. It's not like in London, where it is normal to meet Italians who speak loudly on the street, on the subway, and on buses. After the Second World War, the Italian community in my city, Birmingham, thinned considerably. Lately I've happened to hear Italian more often while I'm shopping in the center. It is a good feeling to catch conversations in your own language while out and about. They come not only from white Italians, but also from Italian girls of African origin who speak, chuckle, exchange phrases and jokes colored by Roman or Neapolitan or Lombard accents.

The Bengalis who run the fruit and vegetable stalls in my neighborhood also speak Italian. They know that I come from Italy and therefore, although we are all able to speak and understand English, it is natural to converse in Italian. They tell me about their stay in Italy; some lived there for over ten years in various Italian cities. They moved to the United Kingdom so their children could study and gain access to British universities.

At Smethwick Library, in the area where the Sikh Guru Nanak Gudwara temple is located, I hear teenage boys, with the typical Sikh turban on their heads, speaking Italian. Intrigued, I asked them, "How come you speak in Italian?" With extreme naturalness they replied, "We were born and brought up in Italy!" All these people are mostly Italian citizens and move around Europe in search of a better life.

A funny thing happened to my daughter Samira while she was having lunch with her son in an Indian restaurant called "Jimmy Spice." The waitress serving them, hearing them speaking Italian, widened her eyes and asked them, "Do you speak Italian?"

"Yes," said Samira. "We are Italian—and where are you from?"

"I come from Novara," the girl replied, frowning.

Samira, taken by surprise told her, "I was born in Novara!"

"What bad luck!" the other exclaimed, and they started laughing together.

## Bull Ring

I'm walking in the very middle of Birmingham: I'm at the Bull Ring, where many tourists take photos of the majestic grumpy-looking bronze bull. They are in the beating heart of the city which always swarms with people so different from each other. They are dressed in all kinds of ways, from the girl in shorts and piercings with dyed purple hair to the woman covered with *niqab*. Street performers are playing musical instruments and singing, others are dressed in costumes borrowed from science fiction films. A preacher with a microphone in his hand challenges the Conservative government.

The sound of *suras* from the Quran fills the air. It comes from a stall that offers booklets which explain what Islam is in simple language but very thoroughly. A copy of the Quran translated into English is given as a present to those who are interested and request it. The faithful present do not pester passers-by with inappropriate and insistent demands for attention or by thrusting leaflets at them. If someone is intrigued and stops, the bearded boys in traditional tunics are ready to answer—in perfect English—the questions they are asked.

How long will I have to wait to see my country, Italy, afford us this opportunity for dialogue?

## Central Library

We Brummies are very proud of our new Central Library. It is the largest public library in Europe.

Seen from the outside, I think it looks like a large, layered wedding cake covered with rings intertwining in alternating silvery and golden colors. On its façade there are large windows. It is very bright inside and offers plenty of space for study and reading. From the huge terrace you can see the square and enjoy a panoramic view of the city. Strolling among flower beds of thyme, oregano, sage, lavender, and rosemary you notice the bright colors of tulips and other flowers that mark the seasons. On the many wooden benches people sit comfortably, reading or breathing in fresh air under an ever-changing sky.

We don't expect to enjoy this oasis of serenity in summer; the important thing is that it is a clear day even if cold or windy. We know that sooner or later, unexpectedly, a shy and mischievous sun will appear. Groups of smiling visitors take selfies. Children run about—without shouting.

I often go to the library. Inside there are open spaces furnished with comfortable armchairs. You can always find a corner to retreat and relax.

I like watching people. They are of all ages. Young students are perched on stools with their eyes fixed on the screens and their fingers tapping fast on the keyboards of their laptops. Middle-aged people are reading newspapers and magazines. All around there is a muffled silence; it seems a place of prayer. And when the time comes to pray, there is a room where I can withdraw, do my ablutions, and offer my gratitude to Allah.

## Sport

Islam does not deny women the right to take part in sport, and in the Olympic Games female Muslim athletes have won medals in various sports such as boxing, fencing, and beach volleyball.

Islam encourages sport, but in Europe many rules and regulations about what Muslim women wear are proliferating, and they make it more difficult for us to dress as we please. For example, the *burkini* has been banned in some pools and some schools have banned girls from wearing the hijab and denied them the right to keep their legs covered during sports. These rules are imposed in the name of secularism: "Only then—when such clothing is banned—can Muslim women feel free," I was told. I believe, on the contrary, that these measures prevent integration and seek to normalize us—make us conform to the norms of the majority—erasing our visibility. These constraints on what we wear prevent some women from participating actively in social life. How does a Muslim woman or girl integrate if no one even tries to see her point of view and to respect her right to manage her body?

It also makes me think that these statements are often made by white Western politicians who claim that they would "liberate" Muslim women from the restrictions imposed on their bodies by their fundamentalist and backward menfolk. Such statements are made without considering the women they are addressing: they have brains, spirituality, and great respect for themselves. Our so-called liberation would mean forcing us to strip ourselves and adopt a model of morality and femininity that we do not share. I also want to point out that this approach has something paternalistic about it, typical of the period of colonial domination, during which it was necessary to "teach" the submissive how to behave in a "civilized" manner.

I honestly cannot understand why Muslim women are prevented from expressing their spirituality in the way they dress while nuns can freely show their devotion by wearing a habit with a veil.

I hope that this bigoted mentality will one day become a distant memory and that we can live in a peaceful climate of mutual respect. Fortunately, after so many struggles, Muslim women can participate in the Olympics while preserving the symbols of their religious identity.

Unfortunately, from this point of view I feel freer in Tunisia or Malaysia than in Italy. Surely after this statement of mine, I would not be surprised if some of the new rulers told me to leave my country and move to the countries I have just mentioned. Why should I? I am and I feel Italian. Italian in my own way.


## Spratton Hall School

A few years ago, I was invited to Spratton Hall School to talk about Islam. It's a private preparatory school, an imposing stone building set in fifty acres of the green Northamptonshire hills.

I find a class of children smiling, polite, and eager to learn. They are about eleven years old and I notice that they are all white. They wear the school uniform: classic trousers with jacket and tie for the boys, while the girls wear skirt, jacket, and tie. They look smart.

Most likely I am the first person wearing the hijab they have ever met. They sit at their desks with pen and notebook, taking notes while I speak. I introduce the five pillars of Islam; I project some photos I took during my pilgrimage to Mecca. I let them hear the recitation of *Fatiha*, the open *sura* of the Quran, explaining its meaning. In the second part of the session the students bombard me with questions, which I answer. They are spontaneous, curious, open.

The time has passed quickly and the lesson ends. They gather around me for a souvenir photo. Smiling, they say goodbye and leave the classroom. They have become familiar with a culture and a religion they did not know.

The teacher tells me that the students were genuinely enthusiastic about the talk. The following are some comments that appeared on the school website:[1]

"I learned that *Zakah* is 2.5% of its income to give to the poor"

"I learned that the rules are not as strict as I thought"

"I learned that being Muslim is not just a religion but a lifestyle"

"I learned that mothers are respected by Muslims"

"Shirin said it is not difficult to fast in Ramadan because her goal is Allah and not food"

"I learned that when Muslims go on a pilgrimage to Mecca, pilgrims wear white to remember that we are the same before Allah"

"We listened to the *Fatiha* and its translation. This is the first *sura* of the Quran. It is important because it is what Muslims recite during their everyday prayer"

This is one of many examples of how important it is to talk with young people and give them the opportunity to ask questions. A little girl made me smile when she asked me if I was going to sleep with the hijab on. Another girl wanted to know if the obligation to fast also applied to children. Their spontaneity moved me, we had fun, and we felt at ease. Only when there can be dialogue and people know and understand each other do doubts and fears disappear.

## British Muslim TV

In recent years we have witnessed major changes in our lifestyle. We not only receive local television, but we can connect via satellite or through the internet with broadcasters around the world. Internet and satellite TV have made it less painful to be so far away from one's own country—in my case Somalia and Italy. With the various applications on computer, tablet, or mobile phone we can not only talk in real time with people we care about, but also see them on our devices.

Satellite antennae have changed the external appearance of our homes. I like to observe them as I walk along the endless streets of red brick houses typical of urban English neighborhoods. They are modest homes without a front garden. Their monotony is a little sad. The satellite dish that stems from their roofs looks like a giant flower, bringing to these homes memories of the scents and colors of distant lands. I too am one of the people who want to have the world within reach of a remote control. Woe to me if I did not have Rai, Al-Jazeera, BBC World, and Somali channel TV!

Digital terrestrial broadcasting in the United Kingdom broadcasts national television programs that interest me like British Muslim TV. This channel offers a varied schedule: cartoons for children, readings of books, games, classes on the cooking of various cultures, news, interviews, recitations and interpretations of the Quran, music and meetings with various Jewish and Christian religious groups who explain their own sacred texts.

It is a channel also followed by non-Muslims because it deals with current topics and interacts with various communities. It makes known the diversity of Islam, debunking the generalized belief that depicts it as a monolithic world closed to those outside it.

I am convinced that if the Muslims in Italy had the same opportunities as Muslims in the United Kingdom, our Italian society would benefit enormously.

Unfortunately, in our country, Italy, voices in the media "outside the choir" are always isolated.

I remember years ago the weekly *Nonsolonero* feature presented by Maria De Lourdes from 1988 to 1994 on *Telegiornale 2*, the RAI 2 news program. It was the first Italian television broadcast dedicated to immigration and racism. It was very popular and conducted by an immigrant journalist. I didn't miss an episode and, like me, millions of other viewers wanted public television service to help them better understand their country. It was a voice that succeeded, in the short space available, in touching on many important themes and helped to eliminate stereotypes. It created a dialogue, introducing viewers to the countries the migrants came from and explaining the work they carried out in Italian society. They tried to give a face, a name, an identity to these people so that they did not remain a formless and anonymous mass of "immigrants."

## Friday

Every Friday the Birmingham mosques are filled with worshippers, women and men of all ages. Some businesses close when people leave to participate in congregational prayer. It's nice to see white-bearded men in their *salwar kamiz*, which stick out from under their coats, and with the typical Afghan hats on their heads, walking through the rain with umbrellas in their hands, hurrying off to the place of prayer. The Friday sermon helps to reinforce Islamic principles and remind the community, in the spirit of Islam, how to deal with certain problems—that is, by creating universal brotherhood and sisterhood.

The small neighborhood mosques are not just places of prayer: after school they offer classes for children who study the Quran and for adults, they organize *Tafseer* classes, in which the various *suras* of the Quran are explained. In the morning older women meet to socialize and to memorize the sacred book.

The Birmingham Central Mosque, the largest in the city, and the Green Lane mosque are busy all year round organizing cultural events and meetings for inter-faith exchanges with churches and synagogues. They work actively for the community as a whole, without distinction between ethnic and religious groups and with the charity Food Bank, distributing parcels of food to needy families. During the winter, volunteers go into the streets of the city to offer hot meals to the homeless. Many mosques join and collaborate with humanitarian NGOs.

A network of professionals, doctors, and psychologists offer the community various essential services, such as family counseling and a service for celebrating weddings. Funeral services that comply with the precepts of Islam are also offered.

The mosques also collect for the annual *Zakah*, to which every believer must contribute. To bless the wealth is one of the five pillars of Islam. Of the goods one owns that produce wealth or that come from productive activities, 2.5 percent must be donated to specific categories of people such as orphans, widows, and the poor. Priority is given to the local community, but in cases of sudden natural disasters abroad, *Zakah* can offer valuable support to the affected populations.

In addition, mosques organize meetings for professional training, where members of the community are helped to compile a C.V. correctly and to get advice on how to look for work. They also offer basic training courses that outline the steps to take to improve one's career and specific workshops at low cost.

Mosques also promote a number of youth clubs that organize sports and recreational activities for boys and girls such as football, volleyball, basketball, martial arts, and cricket. Scouting is also widely practiced.

The women of the community are involved in the Sisters' Coffee Mornings—a time to meet, relax, and be creative at workshops on wellness, crafts, and cooking.

I am part of the Green Lane Mosque community, and every Wednesday I attend meetings to welcome women who have recently converted to Islam. These women are often hindered by their families and need someone to confide in. After some time, you don't just meet once a week, you become friends. Listening has enriched me as a human being by making me understand the difficulty that being converted to Islam presents for the extended family, the converters' community of origin, and the people dearest to them.

Almost all the mosques take part in Open Mosque Day, when the mosques welcome visitors to demonstrate that they are not closed places, dedicated exclusively to prayer, but meeting places that seek to provide for the needs of the local community in an inclusive way.

During the month of Ramadan, the *iftar*, the meal to break the fast, is served in the mosque: water, dates, samosas, fruit, biscuits, tea, and coffee.

I nourish the hope that before long in my country too—in Italy—dialogue between different communities will take place.

## Small Heath Park

In Birmingham, the Eid Al-Adha festival is celebrated in Small Heath Park.

It is the *sunnah*, the custom of the prophet Muhammad, an example to be imitated.

On this day, Muslims gather to pray outdoors. It is the second of the two Islamic festivals celebrated throughout the world.

Eid Al-Adha commemorates Abraham's readiness to sacrifice his son Ishmael at the behest of Allah. It falls on the tenth day of the last month of the Islamic calendar, Dhul Al Hijja, the month in which the pilgrimage to Mecca takes place.

To facilitate the influx of the faithful, some streets near Small Heath Park are closed to traffic. The police are there to ensure safety and several ambulances are parked in case they are needed. The volunteers—boys and girls—wear fluorescent yellow "Hi-Vis" jackets and collaborate efficiently with the police in keeping order. The organization is perfect: nothing is left to chance.

The sight of a flood of people of all ages arriving with cheerful expressions on their faces is spectacular. They chant, in chorus, *Allahu-Akbar, Allahu-Akbar!* Looking around you are struck by the multitude of people you see. They come from all over the world, in many different costumes: the *burnous* stands out—a typical North African garment with a hood, the blue Tuareg *djellaba*, the simple soft white *salwar kamiz* of the Bengalis and Pakistanis, and the elegant and multicolored African costumes.

Men with thick, white and silver beards or jaunty orange beards dyed in henna repeat the *tasbih*—the Muslim rosary—using wooden prayer beads. Boys wear showy red and white checkered *keffiyehs* typical of Saudi Arabia and have their raven black beards cut in the latest style. Young people in jeans arrive in groups wearing *keffiyehs* around their necks.

Colorful African mothers in purple and lavender kaftans, with floral turbans hiding their hair, walk hand in hand with their little girls, who wear dresses edged with gold lace, the traditional dress for a new party. Shimmering satin bows and butterfly hair clips studded with fake diamonds and rubies keep wavy ponytails and long swinging braids in order. The boys wear crocheted hats and jackets with delicate embroidery. Women walk confidently, covered with *niqab* but wearing trainers—and you can just see a pair of flared jeans underneath the black dress.

Many of those present have come from other parts of the West Midlands and have traveled for several hours before arriving in Birmingham.

The powerful megaphones around the park spread the persuasive voice of the imam who leads the congregation. Tens of thousands of the faithful, shoulder to shoulder, silently concentrate in prayer. Men and women synchronize their movements. Simultaneously they bow, stand up, bow again, and rest their foreheads on the ground as a sign of submission to Allah. Last year, one hundred six thousand of the faithful gathered in Small Heath Park.

In the park rides, mini-golf, and stalls for food, clothing, books and balloons have been set up. Henna and face-painting artists make full use of their creativity to meet the demands of the moment.

Friends and relatives enjoy picnics sitting on the grass. Children run in the fresh air and roll around on the ground. Women chat, gesticulate, and laugh as they serve *biryani* (lamb or chicken with rice), *samosas* (meat-filled dumplings), *bhajis* (chickpea flour pancakes), *halwa* (honey sweets), and *ferni* (Afghan sweets) on paper plates. There are also many other desserts cooked with cardamom, pistachio, and cinnamon. New friendships are made. New flavors are tasted. There is a lot of joy. English is mixed with Urdu, Somali,

Pashto, Arabic, Wolof, French, Italian, Albanian, Turkish, Bosnian, and Chechen.

I will never forget our first *Eid* at the park. My grandson Jibril was five years old and was delighted to be dressed up. He wore a beige *thobe* (a long-sleeved ankle-length robe) with a colored waistcoat and on his head a blue crocheted *kofi*. I prepared a large pan of *pasta al forno* and *tiramisù* to share with the people who were sitting with us. Every year the flavors of Italy are combined with those of many other cuisines and brighten up our *Eid* in Birmingham.

## Brexit

The day after the result of the referendum on the United Kingdom's exit from the European Union was declared, I could hardly believe it. It was a traumatic experience that made me realize how, in a democracy, everything that has been painstakingly built up for years can suddenly vanish.

In England it is a subject that is difficult to discuss even within families. It has created a social and political rift that is unlikely to be repaired in the short term. Discontent, disappointment, doubts, and fears have affected the millions of Europeans like me who have felt at home in the United Kingdom. A bureaucratic chaos has been created that has seen dramatic cases of families who are at risk of being sent away from the country after living there for years.

Discrimination against Muslims and people from Eastern European countries has increased.

I am aware of Anglo-Asian families who, carried away by politicians' speeches, voted in favor of leaving Europe. With the victory of those in favor of an exit, they too are now targeted by the extremists because, despite being British citizens, they are not white. The hatred of the right does not spare anyone.

Attacks on veiled women and cases of verbal abuse are happening more and more frequently, and the police are actively collaborating with bodies like Tell MAMA UK—a national project that monitors and offers support to victims of racism against Muslims—by organizing meetings with representatives of the various communities to give them advice on how to protect themselves and what to do in the face of discrimination.

A lot of work is being done in Birmingham toward building bridges. Birmingham is a city created and built by immigrants and is proud of it. Unfortunately, there is insecurity among the various Muslim communities because of Islamophobia. Although in many European countries this form of discrimination is denied or minimized, Islamophobia is a real fact and manifests itself not only in sensational episodes of violence but in daily harassment, acts of microaggression, and insults.

# ~ 4 ~

# Islamophobia

### Hatred

Hate speech haunts the hearts of men and women, the young and the old. Hatred is spread by the megaphones of politicians, by the pens of journalists, by ordinary citizens through social networks. Hatred sows violence: tears and pain divide humanity. History is our mirror, reminding us not to fall into the errors that led to the extermination of entire peoples and to manage our differences wisely. It chills me to see the shadows of the past wandering around like ghosts.

What happens in your soul when you are beaten, insulted, violently attacked?

What happens in your soul when you are mocked, harassed, laughed at on trains, on buses, and on the subway?

What happens in your soul when you are searched like a criminal, cannot get on a plane because you are considered suspicious and are humiliated in front of strangers, colleagues, and family?

What happens in your soul when you read in the newspapers that your religion is violent, and that it is the cause of the problems related to terrorism in the world?

What happens in your soul when television dramas, films, and news programs incessantly describe people like you as enemies?

You disappear, you fade, you are stripped of your dignity. You are no longer seen as a human being.

Sometimes I've been discriminated against because of my veil, sometimes I've talked to victims of discrimination, sometimes I've read their stories and tried to ask myself how I would feel and what I would have done if I had been in their place. I've tried to collect their voices and their stories by reporting them as they were told to me or by trying to reconstruct them from my perspective. They are not sensational episodes of violence; rather, they are much more frequent, everyday incidents, which victims often do not report for fear of being exposed in the media.

## Zena

Zena walks along briskly in her pink sneakers, wearing an elegantly pinned floral hijab. She is at the train station. She's on her way to the university. Suddenly she receives a blow to the back of the head and falls to the floor. She feels sharp pain: her index finger is fractured and her mouth is bleeding. She trembles, she is terrified, and her eyesight is blurred; she sees giant figures disappearing as they move frantically away.

## Jamila

I tremble and hold Jamila's little hands tightly in mine. She is confused, afraid, and sobbing: "I don't know why that man pushed me and yelled in my face: 'Go back to your country!'" Jamila was born in Rome and is only four years old.

## Samia

Samia is twelve years old, but she looks older. She is tall, smart, and self-confident. For the first time, she wears a pretty hijab to school. She is immediately reported by the teacher, and from that moment on she is put under observation: it is feared that she could turn into an extremist.

## Hooriya

My mother is in tears. She begs me, "Hooriya, take off that headscarf, every time you leave the house, I'm afraid for your safety." I reply firmly, "No, mum. Don't strip me of my dignity, of my faith, of my security. They're the only things left for me to hold on to."

## Tarik

Tarik is at secondary school. He is an orthodox Muslim. He is also a lonely and introverted boy. He does not return the looks of his female classmates or shake hands to greet them. He has been taught that this (not shaking hands with the opposite sex) is a sign of respect for women outside the family circle.

I have never denied a handshake to anyone, but I don't think that this gesture should be universally interpreted as a sign of peace, harmony, and respect.

Because of his shy behavior, Tarik is judged to be at risk of becoming an extremist. The school reports this to the government's Prevent program, a controversial Islamic terrorism prevention plan that targets teenagers.

Now Tarik feels different from everyone else in his class. He has always enjoyed going to school, but suddenly he feels alienated and marginalized.

## Muhammad

Muhammad is in his twenties, but his friends call him Moo. He follows fashion and wears designer clothes. He spends his evenings at the disco with his friends. On his right arm he has a tattoo of a blue snake. He's not at all different from his contemporaries, who were born and raised in Italy like him, except that they have the right to be recognized as Italian.

## Amira

I'm tense; a thousand questions pop into my head, and I don't know how my first job interview will go. I shouldn't be nervous: I have a college degree, and I learn fast and work hard. No matter how it goes, I know I can play it on a par with the other candidates and I am motivated. I answer calmly and try to crack a smile, controlling my voice. My interview for that receptionist job went well. The lady looks at me coldly and peremptorily tells me, "If you want the job you will have to take off your headscarf, otherwise you'll scare our customers. This is a respectable hotel."

In March 2017, the European Court of Justice confirmed that employers can choose to forbid their employees to wear religious symbols.

## Laila

France, summer 2016. Burkini have been banned in thirty seaside resorts. At first I thought it was a joke. I read in the newspaper that on the beach of Nice armed policemen ordered a woman to strip because her outfit did not reflect virtuous morals and secularism. The people around her were shouting, "Go home." Laila, her little girl, was in tears.

That summer my family and I were in Tunisia by the sea. I look around, and under the umbrellas I see a mother in a bikini while her daughter is wearing a burkini or vice versa. A lady clad in a black *abaaya* and *nikab*, which leaves only her eyes uncovered, plays in the water with her child. It is a very quiet beach: no one looks, no one comments, no one judges. With a bitter taste in my mouth, I think of my European sisters, and I relish my freedom as I swim lightheartedly in my burkini.

## Warda

Warda is a young journalist. She often travels from North America to Europe. Her big charcoal eyes are eager to take in the world. She wears skinny dark denim jeans, a trendy leather jacket, burgundy velvet boots, and her long wavy hair brushes her shoulders. She is full of energy, like the Moka coffeepot whistling as it boils in the morning.

On this trip, the only thing she adds to her dress is her Blue Tuareg headscarf. In Rome, at Fiumicino airport, she is searched. She is taken to a room and ordered to remove her headscarf. Her long wavy hair smelling of crisp shiny green apples is tied back in a bun and explored by invasive fingers. Warda feels violated. She has lost her confidence.

## Fatima

Her blue uniform enhances the intense color of her eyes. Her authoritarian expression is hostile. Her facial muscles are stiff; two thin lines of purple lipstick draw a slit on her grim face marked by a deep wrinkle on her forehead.

She is holding a passport from a European Union country: it is Fatima's. She scrutinizes Fatima. Looks at the document, turns the pages slowly, slips her passport into a scanner and asks her, "Have you another ID?"

Fatima would like to ask if her passport is not enough, but she doesn't want trouble. She rummages in her bag and takes out her Italian identity card. The woman jumps and runs to her superior. Both scan the documents. He moves his lips slightly.

The woman returns, an expression of disappointment on her face. She returns the passport, slamming it down. Fatima is not worthy of another glance from her.

## Nadia

Nadia has watched many Hollywood movies. The Arab is often represented as violent, possessed, sadistic, brute, depraved, treacherous, traitor, lazy, greedy, and dirty.

Nadia traveled to the Middle East, where she interacted with honest, courteous, generous, and hospitable people. She knows that they have the same strengths and weaknesses as people who live in other parts of the world. She knows for sure, being a Muslim, that *Tahar*, a clean body, is a principal characteristic of our faith. How can she recognize herself in those images? How can anyone recognize her in them?

## Like a Gymnast

I try to gauge the weight of the items of news that strike me every day. I try to walk straight and upright like a gymnast on the narrow balance beam.

I grieve.

 I grieve for every innocent soul who is killed.

 I grieve.

 I grieve, lighting candles on the blood-stained streets of Paris and London.

 I grieve.

 I grieve for the hundreds of people killed in markets, mosques, churches, and forgotten cities: Mogadishu, Baghdad, Maiduguri, Kabul, Cairo. . . .

I am searching desperately for a place where I can light a candle for my dead.

## ~ 5 ~

# Contradictions

### Sister

We met at a bus stop in town. She was standing behind me: we greeted each other, saying, *Assalalmu aleikum*. It was late autumn, and a cold wind was blowing. Her baby girl was asleep in the stroller. She was covered, and you could only see small hands and a little round face peeping out from the blanket. We got on the same bus and by chance we got off at the same stop. We started talking, and then we both turned into the street leading to my house. We lived just a few blocks from each other. "What a coincidence!" we both exclaimed, smiling. She told me that she had lived in Birmingham for a few years, and that she was married to a young Muslim. She had recently converted to Islam. She wore her elegant hijab with casual ease—it coordinated with her plum-colored coat. Her eyes were like the sky on a clear, cold winter day.

Over time we used to meet in the street or at the supermarket. We would chat for a while. The little girl was growing up: soon I saw her walking. One morning I noticed that Khadija was no longer wearing a veil. I hardly recognized her. She stopped and with a heartbroken expression and told me that she had left her husband. Then she added, "I converted for love, but now it's over!"

### The Master

He married her, and told her, "I am your husband, you must obey me."

He became her jailer.
    She couldn't talk.
    She couldn't think.
    She couldn't breathe.
    She became his property.

Brother, remember what our beloved Prophet said: "The best of believers is he who has the best character and the best of you are those who treat their wives better than others" (Zubair 2007, 2, Book 10, Hadith 1162).

### Polygamy

In Mogadishu, during my teenage years, I knew two women in my neighborhood who were married to the same man. Their children played together. They ate together. They grew up together. They were treated with the same care. They had the same surname and were entitled to inherit from the same father. Both wives were respected. They were not the only family of this type; this practice was common.

Today some Muslim men are hiding a second wife. Just as you do with a lover in Europe.

## Respect for Women

Tell the faithful men to cast down their looks and to
guard their private parts. That is more decent for them.
Allah is…well aware of what they do.
—Quran (24:30)

What angers me is knowing that in many countries women are harassed as they walk down the street. There are men who shout from hooting cars, screaming vulgar compliments. Women's bodies become prey to rapacious hands-on buses packed with people.

If a woman passes a bar where only men are sitting, she feels their eyes undressing her.

"Her dress is too tight."

"Her skirt is too short."

"Her makeup is too flashy."

They blame women for their own prying eyes.

The Islamic principle that many brothers forget is the command that Allah has given to men: respect women.

## Internet Dating

In the present age of technology, websites where you can meet your soulmate are sprouting like mushrooms. After long reflection and research Amina subscribed to a dating site for serious relationships. She read many profiles and chose the man who most attracted her.

He is a lawyer in London—Abd-al Hameed Tawwab, a name that contains two of Allah's ninety-nine names: "Servant of the Praiseworthy" and "He who accepts repentance." Thirty-two years old, a practicing Muslim of Afro-Caribbean origin, a convert to Islam. Athletic, he has a clean face with smooth chocolate skin. Connoisseur of Islam, very active on social media and preacher of Islam. Student of Islamic law with only a few exams left until graduation. Passionate about religion, he thinks that the right time has come to start a family.

They chatted for a few months, drawing their plans for the future. They explored and exhausted every single topic and curiosity about each other. Amina was intrigued by the man's discretion. He showed her his picture only once, and then he immediately removed it from his profile. He asked for Amina's photo after weeks of messaging her, unlike most of the "brothers" registered. He never asked her for personal phone numbers and emails. Everything had to be pure, just like the site they were using. Everything was perfect; Amina felt she had found a partner. Even when they decided it was time to get married, he wanted to do things in conformity with Islam, in a pure halal way. He asked for the number of her *mahram*—father, brother, or guardian—so that he could come and propose marriage. He talked to her parents.

Amina listened to the call on the speakerphone. For the first time she heard the man's confident, warm, and mature voice. She was enchanted by his London accent. At the end of the conversation, her father invited him to come to Sunday lunch.

Amina was in love with this man: he was as honest as the light of day. She hadn't slept all night; she was excited. That morning Dad was the butcher's first customer, and he secured the best cut of lamb. Mom was busy in the kitchen grilling eggplant and peppers and preparing spices. The delicious scent of apple tart with cinnamon wafted through the house.

Amina's room was a battleground of *abayas* and hijabs. She felt like a little girl at her first dance. She felt butterflies in her stomach. Everything was ready, and everyone in the family was waiting. Every five minutes Amina ran upstairs to see from her bedroom window if a car had stopped outside their door.

Amina looked in the mirror a thousand times. She changed her lipstick from pink to dark pink. She pinned her hijab with a less flashy clip. She lightened the blush on her cheeks. A touch of mascara. Her hands were shaking.

The hands of the clock were dragging time along like a sleepy snail. Half an hour, an hour, an hour and a half. Dad checked his mobile phone to see if there had been a call or a message for him. He could have been late for traffic, or he could have been involved in a car accident. No messages or missed calls.

Dad tried to call him. A metallic voice answered him. It was a recorded message from a robot which kept repeating: "The number selected is nonexistent." "The number selected is nonexistent."

They all looked at each other speechless. Amina ran to the computer. She connected to the marriage site to check if there was a message from him: no trace of the London lawyer. Amina was in a cold sweat, and she no longer felt her body. She was a piece of ice with dilated pupils. The folder was empty. His name and all their history, their idyllic romantic story and their promises had disappeared from the screen like a sandcastle dissolving into the ocean.

She never expected that a man who presented himself as a devout and Allah-loving Muslim could turn out to be a *mascalzone*—a crook of the worst kind.

## Universal Equality

O mankind!...We created you from a male and a female, and made you nations and tribes that you may identify yourselves with one another...the noblest of you in the sight of Allah is the most Godwary among you....Allah is all-knowing, all-aware.

—Quran (49:13)

Girls are marginalized by their families when they marry outside their community. Mixed marriages are still taboo. We are so trapped in our own little circle. We believe we are superior to others because of our status and the color of our skin. Have we already forgotten the words spoken by our Prophet in his last sermon?

## October 14, 2017

Under the rubble of buildings:

burnt bodies,
vehicles blown up.

There is no time to escape.
There is no time to think.
There is no time to pray.

There is no time to breathe.
There is no time to scream.

On October 14, 2017 in Mogadishu
A terrorist act killed four hundred people and wounded
 hundreds.
The population rushed to donate blood
In hospitals that were not equipped for such an emergency.
They donated food.
They helped to gather scattered human limbs in order to
 give the dead a proper burial.
They ran to clear the streets of debris.
There was no time to stop and cry.

The people of Mogadishu,
my city, which does not give up,
is an example of strength and unity during a moment
 of mourning.

Who are the dead?
They are Muslims.
The wounds I carry inside have not yet had time to
 heal.
Our dead are countless, we are a faceless people.
And a president had the arrogance to forbid entry to the
 United States for those coming from countries like
 Somalia calling us "terrorists."

Tuke the handsome inky black crow
watches the city
cawing flying in the hot salty air
under a *bulug* sky
and big scudding cotton candy clouds

Tuke the handsome inky black crow
watches the city
cawing boldly at the disorderly traffic jam
flapping its sleek feathers above
wobbly yellow *tuk-tuk* motor scooters
and hooting cars and lorries

Tuke the handsome inky black crow
watches the city
cawing and hopping on dirt road
wings sprinkled with reddish dust
pecking stale *rooti* bread and
ripe *canbe* mango

Tuke the handsome inky black crow
watches the city
his persistent cawing from a telegraph pole
intertwines with the voices of
women in busy markets *suugs*
shopping and chatting
noisy children back from school
wearing worn flip-flop *dacas*
and the call for prayer—*dhuhur*

Tuke the handsome inky black crow
watches the city
cawing in agony

Monster, who are you, hiding from under a false flag?
Who gave birth to you?
Let me see your face.
What do you want?

Why do you hide behind a screen to enchant,
to ensnare our youth with false promises
disillusioned from a selfish and ephemeral world?

Why do you make mothers cry?
Do you have a mum?
No, you only feed on hate,
and hatred does not win.

Allah is *Al-Rahman*,
He who constantly floods all of His creation
With Love and Mercy

### Fear

> Whoever kills a soul, without [its being guilty of]
> manslaughter or corruption on the earth, is as though
> he had killed all mankind, and whoever saves a life is as
> though he had saved all mankind.
> —Quran (5:32)

As soon as a terrorist act strikes Europe, the relentless politicians point the finger at my beliefs: "It's the Muslims, Islam is the problem" is heard everywhere.

I feel offended by this mentality because Islam celebrates the sacredness of life. I was brought up with these values.

*

In the morning, before getting out of bed, I hear a voice inside me whispering a wish: "Let's hope that today there is no terrorist attack in Europe."

I am afraid of being seen as one of "them."
I am afraid of those accusing looks that hurt more than words.
I am afraid of having to justify myself as a Muslim.
I am afraid to be blamed for a crime that I did not commit.
I am afraid of the waves of aversion toward Islam that are
claiming nameless victims.
I am afraid of the silence of my colleagues.
I am afraid for my son who goes to school and bears a
Muslim name.
I am afraid for my bearded neighbor who goes to the mosque.
I am afraid for European Muslims.

I am afraid to change.
I am afraid of becoming indifferent to the massacres of
innocents killed across the borders.
I am afraid of these borders, which are suffocating me.
I am afraid of these borders, which are isolating me.
I am afraid to think only of my own safety.

**

Fear is the invisible enemy that darkens our minds
like the poison that destroys all beauty around us.
Fear makes us blind, deaf and dumb.

Fear corrodes our hearts,
like an old, abandoned nail
rusting under the rain.

Fear freezes the minds.
Fear breeds hate,
and kills reason.

***

I remember the chilling scenes of the Ku Klux Klan in action which I saw in movies when I was younger in Mogadishu. A group of men on horseback, all in white and wearing white hoods with only two holes that revealed hateful eyes. They arrive at a gallop holding a fiery cross. It is a symbol that pierces the darkness of the night.

My fear is true, I know that the KKK and other supremacist movements nowadays are still recruiting new followers.

Yet never, ever, have I connected that cross to all Christians.

## ~ 6 ~

# A Dialogue on Memory, Perspectives, Belonging, Language, and the Cultural Market

BY SIMONE BRIONI AND SHIRIN RAMZANALI FAZEL

According to Donald Pease, the relationship between authors and critics has often been imagined "in such a way that the author seemed an effect of the critic's interpretation rather than a cause of the work" (Pease [1990] 1995, 111). It is possible to rethink this relationship by looking at texts as a dialogue between different parts—including their authors, market, critics, and readers—rather than simply a reflection of the author's thoughts that need to be deciphered by critics. The author is not a prophet, and his or her text is not holy, but he or she is part of a constant interpretative and discursive process that involves many people who share their agency, creativity, and competence. To look at the text as the result of such dialogue means not only to change the way we understand reading and writing practices but also to rethink the notion of *impegno* (commitment) beyond the top-down approach of cultural formation (Burns 2001). In other words, to show the dialogue from which a text originated has political implications and aims to locate the activity of professional readers and writers within a broader set of power relationships.

The aim of this chapter is to expand on the dialogue that started in 2012 and led to the publication of Shirin's translation in English of two texts she originally published in Italian: the 1994 autobiographically inspired text *Lontano da Mogadiscio*, which was republished in 2013 as a bilingual e-book called *Lontano da Mogadiscio / Far from Mogadishu*—and in 2016 the English translation of this text was published in on-demand print form by Amazon.com service CreateSpace—and *Nuvole sull'equatore* (2010), whose English translation was released in 2017 in print form through CreateSpace (2017a).

Based on our work together to try and republish these texts in Italian and translate them in English, this chapter shows the difficulties that Shirin has faced in publishing and making her text available. Although modern technology has made it easier to publish and circulate literature, this text argues that "minority" authors still face difficulties in bringing their work to the cultural market. Shirin's texts can be considered an example of "minority literature" because migration literature "has a minor status with respect to the culture and the language in which it has been produced" and "provides a representation of the minor condition of subjects who are discriminated against in terms of race, class, religion, and gender" (Brioni 2015, 7). Shirin is an Italian writer of Pakistani and Somali origins who wears a hijab, and she recounts her autobiographically inspired experiences of discrimination and marginalization. Moreover, Shirin's works were mostly published by publishers that did not have "strong distribution networks" (Brioni 2015, 7). Along with noting the limited circulation of these texts within a national context, it is important to acknowledge that postcolonial literature in Italian occupies a minor role in the global context, which is dominated by literature written in French or English (Ponzanesi 2004, xiv). The use of the term "minor" to identify Shirin's literature refers to Gilles Deleuze and Félix Guattari's concept of "minor literature" ([1975] 1986). Simone has argued elsewhere the extent to which Shirin's work and that of other Somali Italian writers relate to the three criteria that characterize this literature according to Deleuze and Guattari (Brioni 2015), namely "the deterritorialization of language, the connection of the individual to a political immediacy, and the collective assemblage of enunciation" (Deleuze and Guattari [1975] 1986, 18). What is important to denote in this context is that, despite its "'minor' condition," Shirin's literature might have influenced a major change in Italian literature, given that many novels about colonialism have been published since *Lontano da Mogadiscio* was released, and writers publishing with major Italian publishers, like Wu Ming 2 (Wu Ming 2 and Mohamed 2012) and Igiaba Scego (Scego and Fazel 2008), have acknowledged Shirin's influence on their works.

Dialogue is intended in this text as a methodology that can support and help position our artistic practices and scholarly research, respectively. Our dialogue is structured around five key topics—Memory, Perspectives, Belonging, Language, and Market—and reflects on the challenges we have encountered in our quest to make these books more widely available. An important aim of this chapter is to identify key themes in literature about migration and suggest new ways of reading texts such as *Lontano da Mogadiscio* and *Nuvole sull'equatore*, rather than approaching them with the same expectations and questions readers would have when reading canonized texts, such as Dante Alighieri's *Commedia* ([1321] 2007). In other words, a new critical terminology is needed in order to understand the innovative idioms that Shirin and other migrant writers have invented to describe a reality that has lacked representation, such as Italian colonialism, or that has frequently been misrepresented, such as contemporary migrations to Italy.

## Memory

In my novel *Nuvole sull'equatore* the *meticci* are the "Forgotten Italians" that few people know about and who are often considered "outsiders." Despite the prohibition to express themselves in Somali and a strict Catholic and Italian education, *meticci* in orphanages were considered to be different from white Italian kids. Their discrimination needs to be discussed in order to bring respect and justice to those people who have suffered from a racial stigma. The laws against interracial unions and the racial laws disrupted the multiethnic and multicultural social environment of Mogadishu, which welcomed Somalis, Arabs, Indians, and Europeans, among other people.

I have collected testimonies of people abandoned by their Italian fathers and also touching stories of their Somali mothers. Those who have experienced the harsh reality of the Catholic orphanages are real people with whom I am in contact. They were classmates and school friends with whom I have continued to keep relations of affection and friendship. Their mothers were frequent visitors to my house, and they were my mother's friends, whom I used to call "Auntie."

I admire these women, seduced and abandoned by their partners. Amina in *Nuvole sull'equatore* is one of them. They are women who have preserved their pride. Very often they were illiterate, raised in a nomadic world, and inexperienced in life. Once in the city, they were able to adapt to the rules of the new society that surrounded them. In accepting those challenges, they emancipated themselves by becoming involved in political activism and achieved economic independence. In *Nuvole sull'equatore*, Uncle Yusuf symbolizes openness, acceptance, and recognition of a part of Somali society.

I wanted to explain how Italian culture—through school, cinema, food, literature, and way of life—has influenced a whole generation, including myself, of young Somalis who grew up in the twenty-year period from 1950 to 1970. The years to which I refer in *Nuvole sull'equatore* are those of my childhood and adolescence in Mogadishu. Writing allowed me to reconstruct a city that no longer exists.

Another way to reconnect with my memories of Mogadishu is to walk through the Small Heat neighborhood in Birmingham, the city where I have been living since 2010. Many Somalis, especially women, have opened their shops here, and they bear Somali names such as "Afgooye" or "Xamar Wein." The restaurants and cafeterias serve genuine homemade food that tastes of cumin. My favorite Somali mini shopping center is called "Somali Center." It has a cafeteria buzzing with people using mismatched chairs and wobbly tables. Women meet for a quick lunch or a snack. The tea is generous with spices. The walls need new paint, but the atmosphere is friendly and it feels like being at home. Both the ladies who run the kitchen speak with the Benadir accent. They serve *cambuulo*, a typical Somali dish made of red or green beans and sweet corn, topped with sesame oil and sugar. No other place serves *cambuulo*: it is considered a poor dish, but older people love it. The younger generation eats burgers and fries.

Somali cuisine bears the traces of the Italian presence in Somalia. *Sbaghetti* are served with chili powder and bananas. I remember when I was a child *sbaghetti* were very long and had to be cut into half before cooking. They were sold wrapped in thick dark blue paper, which we later recycled or reused. My father was good at building paper boats of different sizes with this paper. *Basta al forno* was commonly served in many restaurants and soon become a Somali dish. With time, Indian spices like cumin, cloves and cinnamon, which are a must in food prepared in Somalia, found their way into some formerly Italian recipes, creating interesting and tasty new dishes. We also used olive oil to fry *cutuletti*. Denizens of the middle class could not do without Olio Sasso—in its typical rectangular can—to dress their salad. Olive oil was also used with a pinch of salt and black pepper on fresh bread as a midafternoon snack. My mother was convinced olive oil had to be part of my daily diet to build strong bones.

This "Italian" food is part and parcel of the emotional background of the people of my generation. I remember that I discovered a new kind of "Italian" food when I moved to Novara in 1971. This is a land of rice production, and it took me a while to learn how to cook *risotto*. The tiny grains would stick together. The rice I knew was Basmati; a long grain rice, which remains separated and fluffy. I was also suspicious of *gorgonzola*, but now it is my favorite cheese. When Italian friends come to Birmingham to visit, they bring big chunks of it, which we enjoy eating while chit-chatting. Another specialty from Novara, frog legs, never had success with my palate.

Another culinary memory of Mogadishu is related to Christmas. I remember the *amaretti* Lazzaroni, which were sold in tin boxes. They were a treat for many Somalis at Christmas, despite the fact that they did not celebrate Christmas. Somali traffic officers expected to receive the *panettone* Motta, the traditional Italian Christmas cake, from Italian residents. There was a festive atmosphere, and both Somalis and Italians enjoyed their lives together. My generation knows how culturally inclusive our city was, but the young Somali of the diaspora have seen Mogadishu on the news—tragic news—and cannot imagine how life was before the Civil War.

The Civil War has also changed the ways in which Somalis perceive themselves. In September 2014, I was interviewed by Abdisalaam Atoo, a Somali journalist, for his show *Warghelin* on Universal TV. He told me that a couple of days before airing the show he put my picture on Facebook presenting me as a Somali writer, and half of the people commented, "She is not Somali, her features and her name are not Somali." Abisalaam was very provocative and replied, "How do we know if a person is Somali? Only because the skin color is different, the hair texture is different? Let us come out of our ignorance and accept the other people who are Somali like us. Only then we can move forward." The interview was entirely in Somali, we talked about how multicultural and multiethnic Mogadishu once was. This kind of discussion gives me hope that things will change in Somalia.

The new generation of the diaspora going back to Somalia brings positive changes to the country. They carry the seeds of a broad mentality and inclusivity. They think out of the box. This will help our future society to progress.

When I left Mogadishu in the seventies, the new military government nationalized foreign companies. My husband was an Italian citizen and had to leave the country, just like so many other Italians. The Italian government gave them refugee status. My father kept his Pakistani nationality and faced the same fate. He and my mother had to leave the city they loved the most with broken hearts. What seemed so tragic at that time turned out to be a blessing. My children grew up having my parents in the same house where they were born in Italy. In Novara, we were the only Brown family, and for my little girls to have *i loro nonni* like the other Italian children gave them the sense of being settled and belonging to a family. From my parents they treasured lullabies, bedtime stories, memories, and heritage to build their future identity, to make them strong in who they are and from where they come. [SRF]

It can be argued that a defining characteristic of the legacy of Italian colonialism is, paradoxically, the absence of memory of this very endeavor in Italy. Even fewer people probably remember that Italy was given a trusteeship administration of Somalia, its former colony, from 1950 to 1960. The Amministrazione Fiduciaria Italiana della Somalia (AFIS) is a unique case within the context of African decolonization, as it was a colonialism limited in time, during which the Italian government controversially gave the previous fascist administrators the task to lead this African country to democracy and independence (Mohamed Issa Trunji 2015; Morone 2011).

Luca Guadagnino's documentary on the topic, *Inconscio Coloniale* (Colonial unconscious) (2011), is one of several works that portray this colonial forgetfulness as a sort of unconscious removal. An example of this "unconscious" forgetting is demonstrated in the adoption of specific colonial terms without realizing the origin of them, such as the use of the term *ascaro* in the media to indicate "mercenary" politicians, such as those who supported Silvio Berlusconi's fourth government in 2010 (Redazione La Repubblica 2010; Redazione La Stampa 2010). I believe that this term was used by many without being aware that it refers to Eritreans and Somalis fighting colonial wars for the Italian government. A similar example is present in Italian street names, which celebrate colonialism, although many Italians are not aware of the histories these street names carry with them (Brioni 2022a, 151–58). This practice has been contested in Bologna, where activists have renamed the streets in the Cirenaica neighborhood after members of Italian, Libyan, and Slovenian resistance movements to Italian fascism (Resistenze in Cirenaica 2016a, 2016b).

Gabriele Proglio has criticized the idea of Italian colonial legacy as an "amnesia," and he has defined this forgetfulness as "selective" (2015). This definition is not set against that which sees forgetfulness as unconsciousness, as historical memory depends on different factors such as education, family histories, and class. The understanding of Italian selective forgetfulness of its colonial past emphasizes the agency of some who purposely use colonial undertones or directly refer to that experience in order to support Italy's military interventions in Iraq (2003–2006), Afghanistan (2001–2021), and Libya (2011), or to discriminate against Muslim minorities in Europe.[1] For instance, Renato Besana's documentary *Italia, Islam. Dalla guerra di Libia a Nassirya* (Italy, Islam. From the war in Libya to Nassirya) (2005) associates the war in Iraq to the Italian conquest of Libya in 1911, celebrating continuity in the Italian civilizing mission of the Middle East. On March 11, 2016—while I was writing this text—the Italian minister of Defense invoked an Italian intervention in Libya as a focal point for a NATO involvement "because of the close historical, cultural, economic, and geographic ties we have with Libya" (De Giovannangeli 2016).

Other signs of this selective memory can be found in the food industry. Karen Pinkus has clearly shown the importance of African bodies and presences and the allusion to colonialism in order to advertise food products during fascism (1995, 22–81). Bananas and coffee were the two main products coming from the colonies that were advertised (Scarpellini 2012, 126–133). Futurist writers Filippo Tommaso Marinetti and Luigi Colombo, known as Fillìa, proposed a "drum roll colonial fish" in their book of recipes (Marinetti and Fillia 1932, 145–146), and Marinetti even wrote a text proposing an Italian imperial cuisine ([1938] 2015, 183–185).[2] Many products celebrate colonialism, including the "tripolini," "africanetti" or "faccette nere" cookies, "Menelik" digestif, and "Ruwenzori" liquor (Abbattista 2003, 1). Guido Abbattista traced the origin of the name of the "Assabesi" chocolate cookies and licorice back to 1884; the name celebrates the great attraction of the 1884 Italian General Exposition of Turin: people coming from the former colonies were displayed as if they were animals in a zoo (2003, 1). These names were obviously used to objectify Africans, therefore treating them as if they were lacking the distinguishing features of human beings (Nussbaum 1995, 256–257).

The companies De Cecco and La Molisana produce two kinds of pasta called, respectively, *tripolini* and *tripoline* (Tripolitans). La Molisana's advertisement argues that the name of this pasta "evokes faraway places, exotic, with a colonial taste," thus identifying the pleasure that consumers should feel by eating the Libyan "enemy." La Molisana even explicitly alludes to the sexual promises of the colonies in the advertisement of its *Abissine rigate* (furrowed Abyssinians), commonly known as "shells," a pasta "of a Fascist flavor . . . they have a soft and welcoming shape, like a bowl, the exterior is grooved and rough, while the interior is smooth. They are perfect for fresh vegetable sauces." The beautiful Abyssinian—an Ethiopian woman who is available for the conquest of Italian men—was a common trope used during the colonial period to incite men to go to Africa and is present in one of the most famous songs of Italian Fascism, "Faccetta Nera" (Blackface) (Scego 2015). And the name "Eritrea" was used in Luigi Comencini's 1964 short movie of the same name to indicate a prostitute, implying that its audience would make a similar association. These descriptions show not only that food is actively used to shape the notion of Italianness, but also that references to a romanticized colonial period can be understood by a large audience in order to sell a product. The use of food to determine the boundaries of the nation is not surprising: ironically, the "slippery" qualities of pasta had been used at the beginning of the century to discriminate against Italian migrants to the United States, where this product was not popular and widespread as it is today (Gardaphé and Wenying Xu 2007, 6).

However, to look at forgetfulness exclusively by Italians in relation to the colonial period would be reproducing a rather colonial gaze on Somalia. There is also a Somali "forgetfulness" about Italian colonialism. Indeed, it is hard for some of the Somalis whom I have met to remember the history of a city that has been completely destroyed. Given that the physical space of this city has been demolished, Mogadishu exists in their memories only as an absent place. *Nuvole sull'equatore* can be seen as testimony to the multicultural environment that was present in Mogadishu before the Civil War. Shirin's *meticcio* narrative illustrates a multifaceted portrayal of the legacy of the trusteeship period both in Italy and in Somalia. [SB]

## Perspectives

"Why didn't you like Torino?"
"People give you nasty looks over there. They are very mistrustful toward Muslims. I stayed for one month at my cousin's house. They would like to leave the country, but their children grew up in Italy and are reluctant to move"
(Shirin 2017b, 107).

### UNDERGROUND

People stealthily checking
A suspect face
Fear plays nasty games
Young male
Thick black beard
Brown skin tone
Carrying a rucksack
The enemy is among us.
Squeezed in a whiff of hostility
A young woman prays in silence
For her safe return home
Her headscarf is a heavy flag to carry. (Shirin 2017e, 37)

In *Nuvole sull'equatore*, I was not very interested in representing the character of Guido, the Italian colonizer. It seemed to me that his perspective was easy to identify with for my audience. I imagine Guido inhaling his cigarette and looking at the city below. From the terrace, looking at the neighborhood, he does not realize that Amina had changed. However, Amina learned how to raise her voice, to look him in the eyes. Her true nature blossomed. Deep in his heart he harbored hate and love for this woman. Was it real love? She was slipping, day after day, out of his power. He was still infatuated with this girl he had met a long time ago, but that girl no longer existed.

While *Nuvole sull'equatore* is narrated through an external narrator, *Lontano da Mogadiscio* is an autobiographically inspired text because I wanted to present my own perspective on migration and colonialism. However, I have been invited to events to represent and talk about "Somali women" or "African women," or more recently about "Muslim women." This brings to my mind the Western mentality of simplifying and dividing people by their ethnicities. Although I live in the United Kingdom with my husband and my daughter Samira, I have kept my house in Italy, where I often travel. My life is still divided between these two countries. Italy is home. My daughter Salima lives there with her children, and I spend my summer holidays with them. From the United Kingdom I follow the news on Italian television and read online newspapers. I chat with my Italian friends on the phone. Am I less Italian because I am a Muslim too? I think an individual cannot represent an entire community. Each one of us carries our own story. We are shaped by personal experiences, and we change every day.

One episode in particular is stuck in my memory. I was part of many panels at a conference in Italy, and I was asked to talk about Islam and women. At that time I was not wearing the hijab, and I felt I could not represent Muslim women. I tried to explain the use of the veil, its religious meaning and obligations. Even if I wear the veil now I still think that I do not represent all Muslim women. Nevertheless, I'm happy to contribute to dismantling negative stereotypes against them, for example, that they are forced by male figures of the family to wear the veil, that they cannot speak in public, and that they are unfit for political life. It is not important which community, ethnicity, religion or gender we represent, but the positive experiences we share with the rest of the world are. This is what makes us part of humanity. [SRF]

As Daniele Comberiati has argued, we can look at the AFIS administration from different perspectives (2018). Antonio Nediani's 1960 documentary titled *Somalia: dieci anni dopo* (Somalia: Ten years later) gives an "institutional" account on the AFIS at the end of the ten-year trusteeship from an Italian perspective. The documentary claims that "Italians have given Somalis much more than they have received," and it represents Somalia through colonial tropes such as lingering on images of wild animals and arguing that Somalis are "slaves to their land and herd."

Another perspective is offered by Enrico Emanuelli's *Settimana nera* (Black week) (1961) and of Giorgio Moser's movie that was based on the novel *Violenza segreta* (Secret violence) (1963).[3] The main character and narrator of *Settimana nera* is an Italian settler who falls in love with Regina, the Somali concubine and servant of a countrymate named Farnenti. Unlike the main character, Farnenti was in Somalia before the AFIS and represents an old-fashioned kind of colonialist. According to Pietro Dallamano, Farnenti is different from the main character since the latter shows a new kind of colonializing attitude, which is "more subtle and more fake. White people find it in themselves, and it works like a woodworm, it is impossible to get rid of it even when they want to be brothers and sisters of those of all races" (qtd. in Pagliara 2001, 134). The more Emanuelli's novel progresses, the more the main character realizes how similar he is to Farnenti (Emanuelli 1961, 201). While the main character morally condemns the brutal colonialist Farnenti, he himself wants to possess Farnenti's woman, and he looks at her as "a tourist who is visiting a museum" (35). It can be argued that while the movie and novel take on a voyeuristic gaze to challenge Italian colonialism, the movie does nothing to reverse the gaze, or show what Regina thinks or feels: she remains an object. In *Violenza segreta* the actress interpreting Regina is referred to as "Maryam," without even acknowledging her full name.

Shirin uses an external narrator in *Nuvole sull'equatore*, and we follow Giulia and her mother Amina closely and sympathetically. Reading *Nuvole sull'equatore* forces us to take a look at the AFIS administration from a Somali perspective, reversing the gaze from the dominant European and Eurocentric perspective. This aspect characterizes Shirin's entire production. For instance, *Lontano da Mogadiscio* and the poem "Underground" invite readers to take a marginal position and imagine what a Muslim might feel in an Islamophobic Italy.

As Chimamanda Ngozi Adichie argues, when dealing with colonial legacies and postcolonial identities, one should always listen to more than one story and consider different perspectives (2009). She underlines the role of power in deciding "how [stories] are told, who tells them, when they're told, how many stories are told." Moreover, she argues that she did not feel able to represent herself and her reality in writing until she started reading African instead of European literature—after which she realized that people like her could exist in literature. This comment is important to conclude my short summary of how the Italian trusteeship administration has been represented in literature for at least three reasons. First, it was not until the 2000s—thanks to novels like *Lontano da Mogadiscio*, Wu Ming 2 and Antar Mohamed's *Timira* (2012), and Igiaba Scego's *Oltre Babilonia* (Beyond Babylon) (2005), and short stories like Kaha Mohamed Aden's "Nonno Y e il colore degli alleati," included in the collection *Fraintendimenti* (Mis-understandings) (2010)—that Italian readers were able to read more than one version of the story. Second (and consequently), it was not until very recently that Italians coming from former colonies could see themselves as subjects rather than objects of representation. Third, reading texts written in Italian can offer only a partial picture of the Italian legacy in Somalia. I hope future studies will complete this analysis by looking at texts in other languages that are spoken by Somalis in the Horn of Africa, including Somali, English, Amharic, and French, and also by the members of the Somali diaspora around the globe. [SB]

## Belonging

My sense of belonging does not confine me to one country, one continent, one ethnic group. I feel comfortable with people with different creeds and nationalities; maybe it's because I have traveled and lived in different parts of the world, including Italy, Kenya, and the United Kingdom. Nonetheless, many people keep asking me, "Where are you from?" The obvious answer is the city where I live, but they are not satisfied by my answer. "Where are you from *originally*?" "Where were you born?" "Where are your parents from?" They always try to strip off all the layers of my identity, and I feel I have to justify my own existence.

My belonging to Italy has deep roots because I speak and write in Italian, which is part of the colonial legacy of the Italian presence in Somalia. I was eighteen years old when I first held my Italian passport: I was able to vote, and I got involved not only emotionally but also juridically with this country. In that very moment, I felt I belonged to Italian culture. In Italy I have raised my daughters and buried my parents. My grandchildren are growing up there.

Unfortunately, the majority of my fellow citizens do not accept me as an Italian. When I say I am Italian, they say, "You do not look Italian." Why is a person of my color always considered an immigrant in my country, and why is she associated with people who bring criminality, drugs, prostitution, and terrorism?

Twenty years back I was traveling to Rome by train. I asked the man sitting in the compartment if the seat next to him was vacant. He looked at me in a judgmental way and replied, "Yes, it is vacant, but this is first class!" It shocked me to see that this man assumed in his little brain that a person of color was poor and could not afford a first class ticket. Calmly, I responded, "I have a first class ticket!"

Things have not changed much today in Italy. It annoys me when Italian officers at customs give that suspicious look and scrutinize my passport as if I have stolen it. Last summer I went on vacation to Tunisia, and on my way back to the Venice airport, I made a stopover at Rome's Fiumicino airport. I was approached by a policewoman who asked me in English, "Do you speak English?" At my affirmative answer, she intimated, "Follow me!" It was like receiving a bucket of cold water in my face. I knew where she was taking me; many of my friends told me how embarrassed and humiliated they felt at Fiumicino when they were asked to take off their hijabs. Several times I have wondered how I would react if the same happened to me, and I tried to mentally prepare for this scenario. Nonetheless, everything happened so fast at Fiumicino that I was caught off guard. I was numb. I followed this woman, and before entering the searching room I told her in Italian, "I know. You want me to take off my hijab!" Her jaw dropped. As I was not prepared to follow her orders, she was surprised that I was defending my dignity. I stripped my headscarf and ran my fingers through my hair before she could touch me. "I have nothing to hide," I said. She was embarrassed: "*Signora*, we are not lawmakers." Showing a fake smile, I put my hijab back on my head: "Would you be so kind to tell your superiors that Muslim women have a bright brain under their headscarf?" Spontaneously, I kissed her on the cheek and left the room. Until now I have not realized how I came up with that reaction, how these words came out of my mouth. I was very upset, but not at her. She was doing her job. This kind of experience left me violated. It is not easy to explain how I feel about it; I can just say that it stays with me. I hope that the policewoman remembers my words.

I get that same unwanted attention in the United Kingdom. In Birmingham, I had felt comfortable walking around since most people accepted my headscarf. However, a lot has changed since the process of the U.K. withdrawal from the European Union began. Muslim women wearing the hijab are now insulted, spit on, and beaten. Their headscarf is pulled off. Hate crimes against people who are not white and speak with a different accent are on the rise. Brexit has created an atmosphere of silent terror that is always in the back of my mind. My rationality and positivity give me the strength to live my daily life calmly.

As an African European person, I feel under threat because of racism, but I also feel the urgency to testify for stories that serve as witness for things that I have seen and that many European and Africans of the diaspora do not know about. In October 2017, I was invited to the Somali Week festival in London. It was wonderful to have the hall packed with young Somalis. Normally it is not easy to gather the youth in one place to discuss and share our work and ideas. Generally, we Somalis meet at weddings and funerals. I read some passages from *Far from Mogadishu* and poems from my book *Wings*. The majority of these youth had not been in Somalia; they were born and bred in London. Others came to the United Kingdom as infants, after the Civil War had already erupted. After the event, many girls bubbling with enthusiasm surrounded me. "*Habo*, you are so cool!" they told me. "I would never have imagined that you listen to James Brown." They were surprised that a lady like me, wearing a hijab, could speak so freely of her teenage years, when she was listening to music, dancing, and going to the movies. I felt like a survivor from a past that would never return. I feel that sometimes we do not tell our kids our stories, as if the war has canceled our history and our lives back in Somalia. Discrimination and the trauma they carry prevent Somali mothers from talking about their own history to their sons and daughters and raising their kids as European Muslims. The fact that many think that "being European" means to be white and Christian shows that Europe is still battling to find its own identity. The fact that I feel less like a "minority" when I travel as a privileged European tourist in Malaysia or in Kenya saddens and surprises me because people do not judge me by the way I dress or I look. [SRF]

The term "immigration" does not account for the many conditions in which a person moves from one country to another. Let me explain this statement by comparing my experience of migration with that of Shirin. Shirin and I have known each other since 2010, when we were both Italian citizens living in the United Kingdom. Some would have considered me an "expat," part of Italy's "brain drain," and Shirin a Muslim or an "immigrant" (writer)—as if she had no "brain" to export, was not residing in a country other than that of her upbringing, and her religion was important to mention only because it emphasizes an irreducible difference between her and those who have other or nonreligious beliefs—thus showing the implicit racism that defines the migratory experience of people of European and African origins.[4] The "brain drain" and "expat" rhetoric is used to cover the fact that Italy is still a country of emigration, and many of its young people have left the country because of precarious job conditions rather than to fulfil their career aspirations or intellectual curiosities.[5] While in Italy, Shirin was often considered a foreigner; in contrast, her Italianness was frequently acknowledged by Italians in the United Kingdom. If I would have still stayed in the United Kingdom after the British vote to leave the European Union, I might have shared with Shirin—although with significant differences due to my white-looking appearance—a similar condition of uncertainty and a similar feeling of being unwelcomed that European "immigrants" may experience in the post-Brexit scenario.

My status as foreigner in the United Kingdom and the United States is characterized by the experience of teaching Italian studies, which made me feel like I was functioning as a representative of "Italian culture" abroad for my students and within the communities where I lived. How could I explain to my students that when I lived in Rome, Romans frequently asked me where I was from (often implying from which other country) because of my accent? My way of approaching or distancing myself from "Italian culture" through an ethnic signifier like food was radically different from the one expressed by my parents. While they would identify "polenta" as the traditional food of our area, the food I miss the most from my hometown Brescia is kebab. The popularity of kebab there is the result of the multicultural nature of a city in which the most common surname since 2012 is Singh ("Cognomi più diffusi?" 2012). I found myself discussing with students how the format of the British television program *Make Bradford British* (2012) could be used to highlight the presence in Brescia of two groups who do not feel exclusively or quite Italian: those (mostly dialect speakers) who in the 1990s supported the Lombard League—a separatist party that demanded the independence of Northern Italy (Cento Bull and Gilbert 2001)—and those who immigrated to Brescia and identify with more than one culture.

Indeed, my identification with symbols of Italianness has been further complicated since I moved to the United States. It had been difficult to explain what symbols I associated with Italian culture to most members of the Italian American community, who came from Southern Italy before I was even born. To keep with examples related to food—an aspect that was frequently used to define Italian identity in the United States (Cinotto 2013)—most of my students' grandparents probably had their first pizza before my grandparents, who told me with excitement when they ate their first pizza in the late 1960s in Brescia, since they moved to this town from a rural and isolated village named Brandico. As "Pizza Hawaii" is present in most pizza places of Lake Garda, I perceive this "foreign" interpretation of a typical Italian pizza as part of my own tradition. Indeed, I spent most of my summers at Lake Garda, where German tourists are so present that some street and shop signs are bilingual.

What some people expect me to talk about as an Italian studies scholar are topics that promote Italy abroad, without redefining what it means to be Italian or interrogating Italy's national identity. However, the research of those who study migration and mobility crosses disciplinary and linguistic boundaries; therefore it cannot be unequivocally associated with one single department, program, or unit within the humanities. [SB]

## Language

Translation and multilingualism are part of my upbringing. I was born in Mogadishu in a mixed family where my parents spoke different languages. My relationship with the Somali language is linked to my land, to my childhood, to my mother. It feels like the sound of a musical instrument that has the magic to bring out my deepest emotions. My schooling was part of an Italian curriculum as Somalia was a former colony of Italy. I consider it my first language. In the years since I spent most of my life traveling around the world, where I picked up different dialects. It has always been easy and natural for me to juggle different languages.

Today I am fortunate to be able to use the Somali language in a cosmopolitan city like Birmingham. I have also maintained friendly relations with old childhood friends, and we still speak in Somali. Listening to news and talk shows through satellite channels offers constant practice and enriches my language with new words. My decision to self-translate my two novels in English comes from different needs. One is the fact that I moved to Britain, although I spent short periods in Italy, where I keep my home and family ties. I had two choices: to continue writing in Italian and have no contact with the country that hosts me or to adapt to the new reality. It is very important to be part of the community where one lives. I love to engage with people, to challenge myself with new projects. Birmingham is a vibrant, multiethnic city that gives me this opportunity. I was selected to be part of a groundbreaking project run by the United Nations Alliance of Civilizations (UNAOC) and the United Kingdom–based partner with the Radical Middle Way Institute of Narrative Growth called "Storytelling for Somalia." It was a retreat for journalists, change makers, and creative people from the Somali diaspora in Wales. It constituted a collaboration between journalism and storytelling with thirty creative change makers from all over the world. It was there, after meeting those very talented young Somali intellectuals, who grew up abroad and had no memories of the homeland except what was passed to them by their parents, that the need to translate my novel *Nuvole sull'equatore* became evident.

It became clear to me that if I wanted to communicate with the diaspora and the world, I had to use the English language. It has not been an easy choice because English is not like Italian with which I have an intimate relationship. Italian is the language that I love and use every day with my family. My relationship with the English language has been as a spoken language during my travels and experiences living in different countries. I have always preferred to watch movies and read books in their original version. At first I did not feel comfortable translating because I did not have the professional tools; I thought about finding a translator, but it was expensive, and also I knew that with a purely literal translation of the novel a part of it would lack its originality. Self-translating my novels is a journey I took with a lot of humility, and I am aware of my limitations. I feel like a little girl who takes her first steps, and I know I'm not ready to run. I have tried in the new language to rewrite and still keep my original voice. In fact, in this new version some words are in Italian. Rewriting and translating helped me to think and write directly in English. Sometimes I feel I am a different person. The publication of my short story, "Foggy Dreams Under the Sun Sunshine," in the anthology *Moments in Time* (2015) by Writers Without Borders Birmingham spurs me to continue. [SRF]

My tongue is like a contortionist
Twisting rolling pulling
That magic muscle
—Shirin Ramzanali Fazel, extract from "Stubborness"
(Shirin 2017e, 34)

Small Italian publishing house Laurana, which specializes in e-books, allowed Shirin's English translation of her first novel *Lontano da Mogadiscio / Far from Mogadishu* (2013) to enter the international market through Internet-based retailers. It is striking that unlike most novels written in Italian Shirin's first novel is available in English, given that—according to a report on all translations recorded in the British National Bibliography, available on the Literature Across Frontiers platform—on average only 3 percent of publications in the United Kingdom (and even lower numbers of translations published in the United States) have been translated from a foreign language in the past two decades. Moreover, this novel was included in the "Reloaded" collection, which—as Laurana's website puts it— aims to "republish the best Italian narratives that appeared on bookshelves between the 1990s and the 2000s, and then disappeared because of the disposal cycles of the editorial system."[6] In other words, the reprint of the book allowed *Lontano da Mogadiscio / Far from Mogadishu* to be acknowledged as one of the best novels of that decade that have gone out of print, rather than as a novel written by an immigrant, as *Lontano da Mogadiscio* was originally presented.

It is interesting to note that *Lontano da Mogadiscio*, as well as another key text of Italian literature about migration, Fernanda Farias De Albuquerque and Maurizio Iannelli's *Princesa* (1994), were published as e-books in 2013. This format gives users the opportunity to look up certain words, thus developing alternative paths of reading. Moreover, e-books allow readers to expand their reading online and offer easy access to additional sources of information such as maps and dictionaries. As Aline Soules argues, "The biggest advantage the e-book offers . . . is the anytime, anywhere accessibility that users love in the database and Web worlds" (2013, 209). A third opportunity offered by e-books is their close relation with textuality, which gives readers the opportunity to easily rewrite the text. To quote Soules again, the chapters of e-books "may be searchable and navigable in a different way from the print works, but other features, such as the ability to 'dog-ear' or 'mark' portions or pages, are print concepts and terminology" (207).

However, selling via online platforms limits the market of plurilingual works by allowing publishers to select just one language for the product description, thus penalizing the audience of bilingual novels like *Lontano da Mogadiscio*. This example shows that along with allowing new forms of publication, e-commerce reinforces the barrier that the cultural market imposes on "minor" and hybrid products. It should also be noted that, as Elizabeth Kline and Barbara Williams argue, the e-book is still seen as bearing a different cultural value than a printed book (2013, 250). Although new opportunities for publication have proliferated, it seems that the chances for "minor" authors to be read and known by a general audience have remained the same. [SB]

## Market

In the early 1990s when the Civil War erupted in Mogadishu, I was very frustrated and felt helpless. My mind could not accept the images of war, destruction, and looting I saw on television. The memories I had of my childhood were colliding with everyday news. The old city had been destroyed; I was losing my past. I started writing the first pages of my book as a diary. I kept it only for myself. It never crossed my mind to publish my diary. My husband encouraged me to share it with very close friends. They found it very interesting, and their support gave me a lot of confidence. They were very surprised to discover the richness and the beauty of my country. They did not know that Italian culture had such a great influence on an entire generation of Somalis. I realized that my story could contribute to reminding Italians of their colonial past and to show a different representation of Somalia, which was not exclusively related to the Civil War.

After two years of hard work, I felt ready to send the manuscript to a couple of publishers. They replied that it did not fit into any of their collections because it was a diary rather than a novel. One early afternoon I was watching *Nonsolonero*, the first Italian TV show on immigration and racism. I had the idea to call them, and I spoke to the TV presenter Maria De Lourdes Jesus. She was very enthusiastic about my manuscript, and she introduced me to journalist Alessandra Atti di Sarro. Alessandra put me in contact with Datanews, my first publisher.

*Lontano da Mogadiscio* was received well, beyond any of my expectations, but the publisher did not support me with the means to promote it. Women's networks, associations working for migrants, friends, and word of mouth were my best allies. Within two years, my book was reviewed in newspapers like *La Stampa, Il Corriere di Novara, Il Gazzettino, Il Giornale di Vicenza,* and *La Gazzetta del Sud* and magazines such as *Agorà, Avvenimenti, Internazionale,* and *Rocca.* I presented the book at schools, universities, cultural events, and political debates in Bologna, Brescia, Milan, Modena, Novara, Padua, Turin, and Vicenza. The audience always welcomed my presence very warmly. I was invited as a guest speaker at a panel within the Salone del Libro di Torino, the most important Italian bookfair. I was the only woman among male journalists talking about the Somali war. It was not easy for me to be on the spot for the first time and to speak to a large audience. I also have been invited twice to be a member of the jury on the first competition for migrant writers Eks&Tra in Sant'Arcangelo di Romagna. In 1996 my husband and I decided to open a tourism-related business in Kenya. We stayed there for eight years. I had no idea the book had such great visibility in academia and influenced other migrant writers. However, I still have no idea how many copies of my books have been sold. Publishers never got back to me when I asked.

Almost twenty years later, migrant writers seem to have fewer opportunities to publish a book in Italy since there are fewer small publishing houses that specialize in this topic. As a consequence, I have carefully evaluated the choice of self-publishing. I took this decision because I needed physical copies of my book, as I am fond of the materiality of reading and I found it surreal to present an e-book in public, without an actual copy that proved its existence. I am really disappointed by the request for subventions to the authors by the publishing houses we contacted. I strongly believe that publishers should invest in the product they want to sell and take the risks of publication. I have never paid to publish, and I want to stick to my principles.

I have always published with small publishing houses. Although I really respect their mission and I am grateful for the opportunity these publishing houses have given me, my books are really hard to find on the market. Therefore, my main concern in order to publish *Nuvole sull'equatore* and *Lontano da Mogadiscio* was to enhance the accessibility of my books to the members of the Somali diaspora, given that the political situation in Somalia has still not stabilized. [SRF]

The fact that works by migrant writers have been mostly published by "minor" publishing companies should not be seen exclusively in negative terms. Some of these publishers encouraged writers to experiment with language, producing texts that cannot be easily categorized within a specific genre and intersperse one or more languages. For instance, the publisher Sinnos produced a collection of bilingual books aimed at young readers called "I mappamondi" (World maps). The authors of these texts are migrant writers who wrote the texts in Italian and in another language they speak. As Graziella Parati argues, "Higher visibility could sensitize readers to important issues about migration, but one could also speculate that a series devoted to migrant writers might set the authors apart in a reductive category marked by isolation" (2005, 100).

Moreover, I believe that these "minor" publications had an impact in the Italian literary market. When *Lontano da Mogadiscio* came out in 1994, there were only a few contemporary Italian authors writing about colonialism. At present, almost every major Italian publishing house has published a narrative text that deals, although to different extents, with the legacy of Italian colonialism. Moreover, writer Igiaba Scego, who started her career with an audience that exclusively included readers interested in migration and colonialism, has acquired popularity and writes books and articles for the general public. These facts arguably show that these texts have an impact on Italian society and culture, although many are still unaware of Italy's colonial history.

A proposal for the publication of *Nuvole sull'equatore* and a book chapter were presented to four publishers from 2014 to 2016. Three of them, two based in Italy and one in the United States specializing in African diasporic literatures, accepted the book with minor revisions but asked for a contribution toward the cost of publication. One publisher that specializes in translation from Italian rejected it, asking twice whether "the book was written well in Italian." This comment is based on a rather outdated idea of translation as a carbon copy of the original. However, I find it interesting, as it shows how the name of the author affects our reading of a novel (Nichols 2015). If an Italian John Doe, Mario Rossi, would have presented a novel to them, I doubt that a publisher would have questioned his proficiency in Italian. A small publisher specializing in e-books accepted the proposal without any cost for the writer, but Shirin decided not to accept their offer because she preferred to release the book in print. If Marco Belpoliti is right to say that e-books are harder to remember because our memory needs a physical space in order to work (2012), Shirin's choice is justified by the fact that her stories testify to tales that have already been rescued from oblivion.

Self-publishing seems a very common option for "minor" writers, although print on-demand companies extract a very high percentage of the sales proceeds for the services of publishing, printing, and distributing. Some examples of those who have self-published are Italian American writer Rose Romano, who published the novel *You'll Never Have Me Like You Want Me* (2016) and the collection of poems

*Neither Seen or Heard* (2016) through CreateSpace. Laila Wadia—an Indian Italian writer who published some of her works with major publishing companies such as E/O and Laterza—used CreateSpace to publish *Kitchen Sutra. The Love of Language, the Language of Love. L'amore del linguaggio il linguaggio dell'amore* (2016), a bilingual text written in English and Italian. The transformation of these marginal texts into commodities of global exchange through publication by Amazon—a corporation whose global cultural influence and ideological homogenization recall colonial dynamics—at best outlines the ambiguities of postcolonial literature, which enact in an interdependent fashion both complicity with neocolonial cultural industries and resistance to them (Ponzanesi 2014, 48). [SB]

## Where We Stand

In an article about Italian postcolonial cultures, Roberto Derobertis asks, "When we talk about the postcolonial, from which point do we—who are working on postcolonialism in Italy—speak? From which place and in which structural and working conditions? From which historical and geographical boundaries? In summary, what is our *location*?" (2014). As we feel it is key to acknowledge and discuss our positions, we decided that we had to break away from the traditional structure and organization of academic articles in order to reproduce our dynamic conversation across continents that was held at a distance. We therefore decided to intersperse our voices, producing a fragmented rather than linear text. Writing about migration not only means to acknowledge the hybridity, which characterizes the texts produced by migrant authors, but also may mean to hybridize the ways in which we organize knowledge, to present a cognitive challenge to the reader, by showing the complexity of multicultural encounters, and to account for the fragmental quality of our experiences within a reality increasingly characterized by transnational connections.

An inspiring project that sparked our interest in sharing our agencies and competences as an activity that could decolonize research and writing practices was called Transnationalizing Modern Languages (2013–2016). This project "investigates practices of linguistic and cultural interchange within communities and individuals and explores the ways in which cultural translation intersects with linguistic translation in the everyday lives of human subjects within mobile and migrant communities."[7] Shirin was part of the project's advisory board, and she has led a series of creative writing workshops, "'I Write with More Than One Voice': Writing across Languages and Cultures," which has gathered poets and playwrights from many different ethnic background and countries, such as Nigeria, Sudan, Somalia, Croatia, France, Bulgaria, and Poland. The diversity of the group enriched the understanding of the culture of the people who live in Birmingham but do not often have the chance to meet each other. The topics discussed included how to represent one's heritage, where to locate one's home, and how to express one's multilingual identity in English. As the Transnationalizing Modern Languages website points out, these interdisciplinary activities are aimed at facilitating a "better understanding and communication between and across diverse cultures" and look at the "role of translation, understood in its broadest sense, in the transmission, interpretation and sharing of languages, values, beliefs, histories and narratives." These transnational and interconnected research practices—which include writers, scholars, and practitioners among other professional figures—offer new resources and theoretical frameworks in order to answer a key question in globalized society: "How do people respond creatively to living in a bilingual or multilingual environment and to identifying themselves as mobile individuals or communities?" Shirin's response to this question was the creation of a poem called "Afka Hooyo" (Mother tongue):

The sounds I carry in my memories:
I live in this bubble of voices—
The sweet warm milk suckled from *hooyo*'s generous breast,
My falling into sleep covered in a blanket of words . . .

My first steps: I wobble, I fall, salty tears ploughing down
    my face . . .
I look at the blue sky,
I stutter, struggle—a funny sound . . .
*Hooyo* laughs—she giggles . . .
She makes me repeat the same word again and again.
Her eyes flicker like the first stars that peep in the inky night.

The sound of this language has memories
Built brick by brick,
It can move my deepest emotions—
The hidden ones
Like pearls buried at the bottom of the sea.
This language is not always
Mellow, pure, soft, musical, kind—
This same language
Can hurt, curse, wound my heart and leave invisible scars:
These guttural harsh sounds can heal my soul.

I carry these notes like a timeless instrument:
I am the howling sound of the arid desert wind,

'The pungent scent of the bush,
The early raindrops of *Gu* and *Dayr*—spring and autumn,
I am the music of camel bells marching toward abundance,
I am the crackling sound of charcoal burning
    *lubaan*—frankincense,
I am the frail sobbing of a moaning tribe,
Of a child crying for help ...
I am the ruthless echo of uninvited bullets,
Of hatred and destruction,
I am the bitter soul whispering prayers ...

I struggle when I have to read this language I love most,
Written in an alphabet adopted from a foreign land,
Signs not strong enough to lift my heavy tongue—
I feel like a ballerina dancing on a broken toe.
I abandon this newspaper,
I refuse to read these words:
*Burcad badeed, burbur, baahi, argagixiso, cadow*—
Pirates, destruction, poverty, terrorism, enemy ...
*Dagaal, dhimasho, dhiig*—
War, death, blood ...

I treasure the language of poets:
*Hooyo's* lullabies,
Jokes and proverbs ...
Blessings and goodness—
*Barako iyo wanaag* (Shirin 2017e, 16)

This poem presents many themes that are dear to those who
have experienced migration: the struggle to articulate one's
thoughts in a new language, the palimpsest of memories and
dreams from the past that populates one's lived experience
in a new cultural environment, and the multiple languages

that are present in one's voice. The text makes its English readership approach Somali words like *hooyo* (mother) not as a "foreign" but as a "familiar" linguistic presence, while it simultaneously shows Shirin's sense of estrangement to pronounce words such as *argagixiso* and *burcad badeed*. While critical analysis has the power to conceptualize the experience of proximity or distance that is involved in experiences of migration, poetry has the power to make us feel distant or close to what we are representing. I believe that this interplay of different approaches, styles, and perspectives is fruitful in order to express an experience that is multilingual, multicultural, and transnational in a coherent text. [SB]

I left Somalia in 1971, two years before the Somali language had a standardized system of writing. I was not educated to write in Somali, and I perceive Somali as an oral language. I feel like the Latin characters cannot lift my tongue properly when I read a Somali newspaper. It is like borrowing someone else's jacket. Too tight and unfamiliar for me. Hearing Somali takes me back to my childhood, when my mother was holding me in her arms while singing lullabies. The same lullabies that I had sung to my daughters, and I now sing for my grandchildren. I associate lullabies with that hug, with physical contact. Many European children who have been raised by a nanny from a different culture have the tune of a particular lullaby still vivid in their memories. Maybe they are not able to remember words anymore, but they still remember the sound, the expression of their nanny, her smell, the expression of her eyes, the sweet sensation of being held in her arms or some little fairy tales from the nanny's culture. "Afka Hooyo" is a lullaby and a prayer for the children who are growing up surrounded by war and violence, hearing words that I have never heard in my childhood, such as *argagixiso* and *burcad badeed*. [SRF]

In conclusion, this chapter has shown that despite the presence of new forms of publications such as e-books, there remain many hurdles for migrant authors to access the literary market and to be recognized as protagonist voices of our contemporaneity. Since literary criticism can have the power—as Shirin maintains—to make "migrant writers" feel like "space invaders" of Italian literature (Brioni 2012, 223), we hope that collaboration between scholars and writers can challenge the "minor" role that authors who immigrated to Italy occupy in the present cultural industry. Subverting the traditional roles of critic and author might be useful to rethink the post- and neocolonial world we live in, in order to show that literature does not transcend social and economic forces but actively participates in social processes and changes.

# Coda

## A Note about This Collaborative Project

### SIMONE BRIONI AND SHIRIN RAMZANALI FAZEL

We believe in collaboration. We have worked together and with others for the production of both artistic and scholarly works. We believe in the power of dialogue to shape antiracist artistic and scholarly research, and to call out injustice and ignorance. We believe that collaboration is difficult but needed. Collaboration hopefully can facilitate the promotion of equality, responsibility, empathy, and mutual respect. In a world in which migrant voices still struggle to find space and be heard, perhaps unifying our voices in dialogue, as racialized minorities and allies, can be a way of making them louder and challenging the structures that exclude and deprive them of access to participation.

Who are our allies? One of the first bits of feedback we received about *Scrivere di Islam: Raccontare la diaspora* was an email written by a common acquaintance, a respected and educated person whose work deals with immigration and refugee rights in Italy. He wrote Shirin, observing that her section of the book seemed to be "an apology of Islamism." Shirin replied that she was actually opposed to Islamism, but this person dismissed Shirin's defense of her intention, saying, "We agree to disagree." In a later thread, Simone intervened and simply reaffirmed Shirin's point. This time the reader "somehow"—we suspect white and male privilege played a role in it—understood Shirin's point and acknowledged that he had misunderstood her point. Despite his role as a cultural mediator, this person did not know the difference between Islamism and Islam, and it took the intervention of a white academic for him to change his opinion. This exchange confirmed the need for a volume like *Scrivere di Islam* to contribute to discussions about Islamophobia. We were disheartened to realize how much Islamophobic language has been normalized in Italian, how widely it has permeated Italian society, and how Simone's ventriloquist role seemed necessary for Shirin to get her point heard.

*Scrivere di Islam* is the result of a friendship that started in 2010, when we both moved to Britain from Northern Italy. Since then, we have built a relationship based on trust, respect, and honest and frank communication. We could also have been drawn to collaborate to feel less lonely while facing a cultural market and an academic environment in which migration literature is not adequately valued or recognized for its important role in helping us understand the mobile and diasporic world in which we live.

Our collaboration was built on the recognition of our own limits and the valorization of the unique knowledge of the other. Simone saw one limit in his upbringing and education, which made him take for granted the invisible norm of whiteness and Catholicism that dominates Italian culture. Collaborating with Shirin and studying her work in her proximity helped him to think about how his access to the means of cultural dissemination could be used not only to discuss literature about immigration but also to facilitate the important reflections and lived experiences that migrant writers have gifted Italian literature with. He believes collaboration helped him understand the intrinsic dynamics of power that are involved in the process of editing, framing, introducing, and translating, which so frequently mediates—and often disempowers and instrumentalizes—migrants' voices in popular media.

Shirin's contribution to the collaboration was her compelling ability to narrate her unique lived experience as a Somali woman in a newly independent country experiencing a unique decolonization process, an Italian refugee from Somalia, an African woman in Italy, and a Muslim woman wearing the hijab in Italy and the United Kingdom. Shirin was born in Mogadishu in the 1950s, during the Italian Trusteeship Administration (AFIS), and she spent her teenage years in Somalia until the military regime took over. In those years, Italy had a strong political and cultural influence in Somalia; thus, Italian culture pervades her memories, education, and language. She came to Italy in 1971 and has seen huge changes since then in what she perceives to be the society she belongs to. She has traveled and lived as an expat in four continents, including Africa (Kenya, Saudi Arabia, Somalia, and Tunisia), Asia (Malaysia), Europe (Italy and United Kingdom), and North America (United States). Thanks to her heterogeneous cultural background and her ability to speak multiple languages, Shirin has known refugees, migrants, and religious minorities whose stories would perhaps not been known if not voiced in her literary works.

In this context, Shirin also recognizes her privilege as an Italian citizen since 1970 who has never known the humiliation of standing for hours in a queue at the police headquarters when a residency permit expires, the anxiety caused by endless bureaucracy, the frustration of not having a house because of the landlord's rejection due to her skin color, and the despair of being deported from a country because she has lost legal status.

However, this privilege of being an Italian citizen is overridden at times by prejudice and racism because she is a Muslim Italian. Wearing the hijab is for her a way to express her religious belonging, and it is a sign for people with interesting stories to tell that they have hopefully found someone who will listen to them. It is therefore sad for her to see that this piece of cloth often carries a stigma and is also seen as an imposition on women. It is unpleasant to be judged for one's clothes rather than for one's intellectual capacities, especially at a time in which women wearing a headscarf, like Halimah Yacob, serve their countries as presidents. What Shirin sees as a symbol of inclusion is perceived by some as a sign of unbelonging and backwardness.

Collaborative practices can be a way of questioning one's beliefs and assumptions, or at least that characterized our experience. Interrogating the sociohistorical, geographical, linguistic, religious, and cultural conditions in which knowledge is produced through a dialogue can be a way to rethink—and, most importantly, challenge—how we create notions of selfness and alterity and include or exclude people based on these categories.

# Acknowledgments

This book was originally published in Italian by Edizioni Cà Foscari with the title *Scrivere di Islam, Raccontare la diaspora*, and both Simone Brioni and Shirin Ramzanali Fazel were listed as authors. Early versions of sections in this book have previously been published in Simone Brioni's "Questions of Authoriality and Literary *Meticciato* in *Scrivere di Islam: Raccontare la diaspora*," translated by Cecilia Brioni, in *Contemporary Italian Diversity in Critical and Fictional Narratives*, edited by Ron Kubati, Marie Orton, and Graziella Parati (Teaneck, MA: Fairleigh Dickinson University Press, 2021), 179–189; Shirin Ramzanali Fazel, "Islam and Me," edited by Jessica Lott and Simone Brioni, *Wasafiri. Magazine of International Contemporary Writing* (2022); Simone Brioni and Shirin Ramzanali Fazel, "*Lontano da Mogadiscio* and *Nuvole sull'equatore*: Memory, Points of View, Language and the Market," in *Contested Communities: Small, Minority and Minor Literatures in Europe*, edited by Kate Averis, Margaret Littler and Godela Weiss-Sussex (Cambridge: Legenda, forthcoming 2023); and Simone Brioni and Shirin Ramzanali Fazel, "'Scrivere di Islam': A Collaborative Project," *gender/sexuality/Italy* 7 (2020), https://www.gendersexualityitaly.com/1-scrivere-di-islam/.

We are very grateful to Sandra Clyne and John Pole, who read the manuscript and helped us to improve it thanks to their useful suggestions.

We are also grateful to Alessandro Vettori, Eilis Kierans, and Sandra Waters for accepting our proposal for *Other Voices of Italy: Italian and Transnational Texts in Translation*, and for their constructive comments and thorough work on the manuscript. Thanks also to all at Rutgers University Press, in particular Christopher Rios-Sueverkruebbe and the production team.

—Simone Brioni and Shirin Ramzanali Fazel

# Notes

## Foreword

1. On this subject, see Burdett and Polezzi (2020). The work springs from the project Transnationalizing Modern Languages, of which Shirin Ramzanali Fazel was a core member.
2. For a recent discussion on the development of Islamophobia across Europe, see Abdul Hakim Murad (2020, 32–68).
3. For a longer discussion of this topic, see Proglio (2020).
4. Francesca Orsini notes in her analysis of the work's success that Rizzoli claimed that *La rabbia e l'orgoglio* was the greatest non-fiction best seller ever in Italy (2006, 445).
5. See also Allam (2006).
6. In Allam's self-representation—to use the language of Homi Bhabha (1996)—the components of culture, society, and person are held less tightly together; the subject who speaks is knowingly constituted through cultural hybridization.
7. His exact words are, "Uno dei luoghi comuni diffusi a livello mondiale è che l'islam sarebbe una religione di pace e sarebbero gli estremisti e i terroristi a diffamarla interpretando arbitrariamente i dettami del Corano. Ebbene, io contesto questa tesi e considero che l'incitazione all'odio e l'istigazione alla violenza siano parte integrante dell'islam dal momento che sono espressamente teorizzate nel Corano" (One of the world's

widespread clichés is that Islam would be a religion of peace and it is extremists and terrorists who would defame it by arbitrarily interpreting the dictates of the Quran. Well, I dispute this argument and consider that incitement to hatred and incitement to violence are an integral part of Islam since they are explicitly theorized in the Quran) (Allam 2008, 69).

8. For example, see Feltri's definition of the threat of an Islamic invasion (2015, 102) or his assertions on women and Islam (60).

9. On what Feltri regards as the totalitarian nature of Islam, see in particular the chapter "Il ritorno del Califfo" (2015, 43–53).

10. Indeed, Feltri's *Non abbiamo abbastanza paura* discusses the perception of the popular appeal of Fallaci (2015, 105).

11. An exemplary contrast with this type of writing is provided by Paolo Branca's commentary on Cardinal Martini's homily (2010). The homily was delivered on December 6, 1990. See also Cacciari (2015).

12. On the adoption of Fallaci's views by members of the Lega, see Allievi (2006, 145).

13. See, for example, Gruber (2003), Molinari (2015), and Quirico (2015).

14. See, for example, the work of Khaled Fouad Allam (2011), Stefano Allievi (2001), or Franco Cardini (2016).

15. See, in particular, Allievi (2006, 53, 85–87).

16. For a brief article on Ghazy, see Provoledo (2007).

17. See Farah Elahi and Omar Khan (2017).

18. On this aspect of remembering, see Hunter (1974).

## Introduction to a *Meticcio* Text

1. In this study, I discussed *Lontano da Mogadiscio*'s major reviews and analyzed Fazel's short stories. As I have written about her literary works in other contexts, some of the ideas in the present study reference articles I have published elsewhere. The list of

publications can be found in the references (Brioni 2013b, 2015, 2017a, 2017b).

2. On Somali postcolonial literature, see Brioni (2015), Gerrand (2016), and Lori (2013). On the literature produced in the Horn of Africa, see Ranzini, Proto Pisani, and Favier (2016) and Comberiati and Luffin (2018).

3. This publication later became available in print, both in English (Shirin 2017b) and in Italian (Shirin 2017c).

4. As part of the Transnationalizing Modern Languages project, Shirin wrote the text "My Beloved Stepmother." See Shirin (2021).

5. On the Italian media's representation of migrants, see Bond, Bonsaver, and Faloppa (2015, 29–200). Among the Italian writers who have discussed Islamophobia in biographical texts, with a particular attention to the role of media, see Takoua Ben Mohamed's comics and Sumaya Abdel Qader's novel *Quello che abbiamo in testa* (What we have in mind) (2019).

6. On women and gender in Islam, see Ruba (1998) and Ahmed (1992).

7. On the concept of "person" in relation to debates about immigration, see Dal Lago (2009).

8. Other texts about Islamophobia in Italy include Proglio (2020), Massari (2006), Sciortino (2002), and Frisina (2007).

9. For an analysis of collaborative texts, see Burns (2003, 2007), Meneghelli (2006), Mengozzi (2013), Parati (2005), Romeo (2018), and Wood (2006).

10. I use the term "second generation" for the sake of convenience and clarity. For a more thorough discussion of the controversial usage of this term, see Thomassen (2010).

11. Both films are currently available in open access through the OpenDDB streaming website. See https://openddb.com.

12. This feature is quite common in postcolonial and migration literature in Italian. For instance, Rino Bianchi and Igiaba

Scego's *Roma Negata. Percorsi postcoloniali nella città* (Negated Rome. Postcolonial paths in the city) (2014) is a collaborative work, made up of an essay by Scego and a collection of photographs by Bianchi, which testifies to the traces of colonialism in Rome.

13. See Brioni (2012, 2017b), Pesarini (2018), and Venturini (2010). Literary criticism on migration literature includes *La quarta sponda* (The fourth shore) (2009), an influential collection of interviews with some of the main women writers on the subject, who discuss Italian colonialism and its legacy with Daniele Comberiati.

14. On the importance of locating research and of collaborative practices in transcultural research, see Wells et al. (2019) and Wall and Wells (2020).

## Chapter 3   Birmingham

1. The text refers to the website www.sprattonhall.com. The comments were published in 2007, and they are no longer available online.

## Chapter 6   A Dialogue on Memory, Perspectives, Belonging, Language, and the Cultural Market

1. In this regard, see Wu Ming's analysis of an article on the sexual assaults that happened in Cologne on New Year's Eve 2016 by the director of the newspaper *La Stampa*, Maurizio Molinari, where he argues that the Arab immigrants who committed them did so because this practice characterizes their culture (2016).

2. Filippo Tommaso Marinetti's *The Futurist Cookbook* is the most comprehensive translation in English about futurist cooking. It does not include the recipes that I refer to in the article, but it mentions other recipes—such as "Libyan Aeroplane" (1989, 158)

and "The Jumping Askari (An East African Soldier)" (160)  that testify to the importance of colonialism in the work of futurists.

3. For a detailed analysis of this novel and its filmic adaptation, see Deplano (2014).

4. On this concern, see Remarque Koutonin (2015). On the criticism of the "brain drain" rhetoric in Italy, see Prunetti (2016).

5. On the data about migrations to Italy, see Caritas and Migrantes (2022). On Italian emigration in the 2000s, see Tirabassi and Del Prà (2014).

6. See www.laurana.it.

7. This description can be found on the website for this project: https://transnationalmodernlanguages.ac.uk.

# References

Abbattista, Guido. 2003. "Africani a Torino. La rappresentazione dell'altro nelle esposizioni torinesi 1884–1911." https://www.academia.edu/2391424/africani_a_torino._la_rappresentazione_dell_altro_nelle_esposizioni_torinesi_1884-1911_.

Abdul Hakim Murad. 2020. *Travelling Home: Essays on Islam in Europe*. Cambridge: Quilliam Press.

Adichie, Chimamanda Ngozi. 2009. "The Danger of a Single Story." TED, October 7. https://www.ted.com/talks/chimamanda_adichie_the_danger_of_a_single_story#t-601839.

Agence France-Presse. 2016. "French Fashion Mogul Pierre Bergé Hits Out at 'Islamic' Clothing." *Guardian*, March 30. https://www.theguardian.com/fashion/2016/mar/30/fashion-mogul-pierre-berge-hits-out-at-islamic-clothing.

Ahmed, Leila. 1992. *Women and Gender in Islam: Historical Roots of a Modern Debate*. New Haven, CT: Yale University Press.

Alighieri, Dante. (1321) 2007. *The Divine Comedy*. 3 vols. Edited and translated by Robert M. Durling. Oxford: Oxford University Press.

Allam, Magdi. 2005. *Vincere la paura: la mia vita contro il terrorismo islamico e l'incoscienza dell'Occidente*. Milan: Mondadori.

Allam, Magdi Cristiano. 2006. *Io amo l'Italia, ma gli italiani la amano?* Milan: Mondadori.

———. 2008. *Grazie Gesù. La mia conversione dall'islam al catto-licesimo*. Milan: Mondadori.

———. 2009. *Europa Cristiana Libera: La mia vita tra verità e libertà, fede e ragione, valori e regole*. Milan: Mondadori.

Allievi, Stefano. 2001. *La tentazione della guerra*. Milan: Zelig.

———. 2006. *Niente di personale, Signora Fallaci: Una trilogia alternativa*. Reggio Emilia: Alberti.

Amara Lakhous. 2010. *Divorzio all'islamica a viale Marconi*. Rome: E/O.

Appadurai, Arjun. 1996. *Modernity at Large: Cultural Dimensions of Globalization*. Minneapolis: University of Minnesota Press.

Atti Di Sarro, Alessandra. 1994. "Introduzione." In *Lontano da Mogadiscio*, by Shirin Ramzanali Fazel, 8–10. Rome: Datanews.

Belpoliti, Marco. 2012. "Perché non ricordo gli ebook?" *Doppiozero*, July 9. http://www.doppiozero.com/materiali/fuori-busta/perche-non-ricordo-gli-ebook.

Bhabha, Homi K. 1996. "Culture's In-Between." In *Questions of Cultural Identity*, edited by Stuart Hall and Paul du Gay, 53–60. London: Sage.

Bhambra, Gurminder K., Dalia Gebrial, and Kerem Nisancioglu, eds. 2018. *Decolonising the University*. London: Pluto.

Bianchi, Rino, and Igiaba Scego. 2014. *Roma Negata. Percorsi postcoloniali nella città*. Rome: Ediesse.

Bond, Emma. 2018. *Writing Migration through the Body*. New York: Palgrave Macmillan.

Bond, Emma, Guido Bonsaver, and Federico Faloppa, eds. 2015. *Destination Italy: Representing Migration in Contemporary Media and Narrative*. Oxford: Peter Lang.

Branca, Paolo. 2010. *"Noi e l'islam": vent'anni dopo*. Padua: Edizioni Messaggero.

Brioni, Cecilia, and Simone Brioni. 2018. "Interdisciplinarity and Collaborative Writing in the Humanities: Lara Saint Paul and the Performativity of Race." *Interdisciplinary Italy*, May 22.

https://www.academia.edu/36717610/Interdisciplinarity_and
_Collaborative_W_vity_of_Race_Interdisciplinary_Italy_pdf.

Brioni, Simone. 2012. "Orientalism and Former Italian Colonies:
An Interview with Shirin Ramzanali Fazel." In *Orientalismi
italiani*, vol. 1, edited by Gabriele Proglio, 215–225. Turin:
Antares.

———. 2013a. "Pratiche 'meticce': Narrare il colonialismo italiano
'a più mani.'" In *Postcoloniale italiano: Tra letteratura e storia*, edited
by Franca Sinopoli, 89–119. Latina: Novalogos.

———. 2013b. "'A Dialogue That Knows No Border between
Nationality, Race or Culture': Themes, Impact and the Critical
Reception of *Far from Mogadishu*." In *Lontano da Mogadiscio /
Far from Mogadishu*, by Shirin Ramzanali Fazel, 361–389. Milan:
Laurana.

———. 2014. "Across Languages, Cultures and Nations: Ribka
Sibhatu's *Aulò*." In *Italian Women Writers, 1800–2000: Boundaries, Borders and Transgression*, edited by Patrizia Sambuco,
123–142. Madison, NJ: Fairleigh Dickinson University Press.

———. 2015. *The Somali Within: Language, Race and Belonging in
"Minor" Italian Literature*. Cambridge: Legenda.

———. 2017a. "Gli italiani dimenticati: 'meticciato' e l'eredità del
colonialismo in Nuvole sull'equatore." Translated by Cecilia
Brioni. In *Nuvole sull'equatore. Gli italiani dimenticati. Una storia*,
by Shirin Ramzanali Fazel and Ramzanali Fazel, 207–216.
Scotts Valley, CA: CreateSpace.

———. 2017b. "Letteratura oltre i confini. *Clouds over the Equator:
A Forgotten History* e *Wings* di Shirin Ramzanali Fazel." *Nazione
Indiana*, July 19. https://www.nazioneindiana.com/2017/07/19
/letteratura-oltre-confini-clouds-over-the-equator-forgotten
-history-wings-shirin-ramzanali-fazel/.

———. 2020. "Scritture Meticce—Narrazioni Diasporiche." In
*Scrivere di Islam. Raccontare la diaspora*, by Simone Brioni and
Shirin Ramzanali Fazel, 13–36. Venice: Cà Foscari Edizioni.

———. 2022a. *L'Italia, l'altrove. Luoghi, spazi e attraversamenti nel cinema e nella letteratura sulla migrazione.* Venice: Cà Foscari Edizioni.

———. 2022b. "On the Making of *Maka*: Collaborative Practices, Autotheory, and Diversity, Inclusion and Filmmaking." *The Italianist* 42(2): 197–210. https://doi.org/10.1080/02614340.2022.2129489.

Brioni, Simone, Marie Orton, Graziella Parati, and Gaoheng Zhang. 2022. "Introduction: Diversity, Decolonization and Italian Studies." *Italian Studies in Southern Africa* 35(1), 1–28.

Brioni, Simone, and Shirin Ramzanali Fazel. 2020a. "'Scrivere di Islam': A Collaborative Project." *gender/sexuality/Italy* 7. https://www.gendersexualityitaly.com/1-scrivere-di-islam/.

———. 2020b. *Scrivere di Islam: Raccontare la diaspora.* Venice: Cà Foscari Edizioni.

Brook, Clodagh and Monica Jansen. 2022. "Transnational Perspectives on Postsecular Italy: Arts, Media, and Religion." In *Italian Studies Across Disciplines: Interdisciplinarity, New Approaches, and Future Directions*, edited by Marco Ceravolo and Anna Finozzi, 93–128. Rome: Aracne.

Burdett, Charles. 2016. *Italy, Islam and the Islamic World: Representations and Reflections, from 9/11 to the Arab Uprisings.* Oxford: Peter Lang.

Burdett, Charles, and Loredana Polezzi. 2020. "Introduction." In *Transnational Italian Studies*, edited by Charles Burdett and Loredana Polezzi, 1–21. Liverpool: Liverpool University Press.

Burns, Jennifer. 2001. *Fragments of Impegno: Interpretations of Commitment in Contemporary Italian Narrative, 1980–2000.* Leeds: Northern University Press.

———. 2003. "Frontiere nel testo. Autori, collaborazioni e mediazioni nella scrittura italofona della migrazione." In *Borderlines. Migrazioni e identità nel Novecento*, edited by Jennifer Burns and Loredana Polezzi, 203–212. Isernia: Cosmo Iannone Editore.

———. 2007. "Outside Voices Within: Immigration Literature in Italian." In *Trends in Contemporary Italian Narrative 1980–2007*, edited by Ania Gillian and Ann Hallamore Caesar, 136–154. Newcastle: Cambridge Scholars.

———. 2013. *Migrant Imaginaries: Figures in Italian Migration Literature*. Oxford: Peter Lang.

Burns, Jennifer, and Derek Duncan. 2022. *Transnational Italian Studies: A Handbook*. Liverpool: Liverpool University Press.

Cacciari, Massimo. 2015. "Introduction." In *Figli di Abramo: Noi e l'Islam*, by Carlo Maria Martini, 1–10. Brescia: La Scuola.

Calvani, Vittoria. 2017. *Incontra la Storia. Fatti e personaggi del Medioevo*. Vol. 1. Milan: Mondadori.

Campbell, Ian. 2017. *The Addis Ababa Massacre. Italy's National Shame*. New York: Hurst.

Cardini, Franco. 2016. *L'Islam è una minaccia (falso!)*. Rome: Laterza.

Caritas and Migrantes. 2022. *XXXI Rapporto Immigrazione 2022*. Rome: Caritas.

Cento Bull, Anna, and Mark Gilbert. 2001. *The Lega Nord and the Politics of Secession in Italy*. Basingstoke: Palgrave.

Cinotto, Simone. 2013. *The Italian American Table: Food, Family, and Community in New York City*. Urbana: University of Illinois Press.

Clericetti, Carlo, 2016. "Ti insegno l'ignoranza." *La Repubblica*, January 9. https://clericetti.blogautore.repubblica.it/2016/01/09/tiinsegno-lignoranza/.

"Cognomi più diffusi? A Brescia Singh batte Ferrari." 2012. *Giornale di Brescia*, April 17. https://www.giornaledibrescia.it/brescia-e-hinterland/cognomi-pi%C3%B9-diffusi-a-brescia-singh-batte-ferrari-1.1164440.

Comberiati, Daniele. 2009. *La quarta sponda. Scrittici in viaggio dell'Africa coloniale all'Italia di oggi*. Rome: Caravan.

———. 2018. "Decolonization: Representing the Trusteeship Administration in Somalia." In *The Horn of Africa and Italy: Colonial, Postcolonial and Transnational Cultural Encounters*, edited by Simone Brioni and Shimelis Bonsa Gulema, 193–215. Oxford: Peter Lang.

Comberiati, Daniele, and Xavier Luffin, eds. 2018. *Italy and the literatures from the Horn of Africa (Ethiopia, Eritrea, Somalia, Djibouti)*. Rome: Aracne.

Comberiati, Daniele, and Bieke Van Camp. 2018. "La figura del coautore nelle letterature testimoniali in Italia." *Incontri. Rivista europea di studi italiani* 33 (1): 89–104.

Cupitt, Dan. 2015. *Ethics in the Last Days of Humanity*. Salem, OR: Polebridge Press.

Dal Lago, Alessandro. 2009. *Non-persons: The Exclusion of Migrants in a Global Society*. Translated by Marie Orton. Milan: IPOC Press.

De Cesare, Chiara, and Ann Rigney. 2014. *Transnational Memory: Circulation, Articulation, Scales*. Berlin: De Gruyter.

De Giovannangeli, Umberto. 2016. "Pinotti, Libia: 'Non vogliamo andare in guerra. Priorità è formare un governo.'" *GrNet.it Informazioni sicurezza e difesa*, March 11. http://www.grnet.it /newsdifesa/7793-pinotti-libia-lnon-vogliamo-andare-in-guerra -priorita-e-formare-un-governo.

De Girolamo, Carla, Mohamed Bouchane, and Daniele Miccione. 1990. *Chiamatemi Alì*. Milan: Leonardo.

Del Boca, Angelo. 1976–1984. *Gli italiani in Africa orientale*. 4 vols. Rome: Laterza.

Deleuze, Gilles, and Félix Guattari. (1975) 1986. *Kafka: Toward a Minor Literature*. Translated by Dana Polan. Minneapolis: University of Minnesota Press.

Dell'Oro, Erminia. 1991. *L'abbandono: una storia eritrea*. Turin: Einaudi.

Deplano, Valeria. 2014. "*Settimana nera* e *Violenza segreta*. Denuncia e rimozione dell'eredità coloniale negli anni Sessanta." In *Subalternità Italiane. Percorsi di ricerca tra letteratura e storia*, edited by Valeria Deplano, Lorenzo Mari, and Gabriele Proglio, 121–138. Rome: Aracne.

Derobertis, Roberto. 2014. "Da dove facciamo il postcoloniale? Appunti per una genealogia della ricezione degli studi postcoloniali nell'italianistica italiana." *Postcolonialitalia.it*, February 17. http://www.postcolonialitalia.it/index.php?option=com _content&view=article&id=56:da-dove-facciamo-il -postcoloniale&catid=27:interventi&Itemid=101&lang=it.

Dixon, Tom, et al. 2018. "Un'Italia frammentata: atteggiamenti verso identità nazionale, immigrazione e rifugiati in Italia." Social Change Initiative, August. https://www.ipsos.com/sites /default/files/ct/publication/documents/2018-08/italyitfinal _digital.pdf.

Emanuelli, Enrico. 1961. *Settimana nera*. Milan: Mondadori.

Fallaci, Oriana. 2001. *La rabbia e l'orgoglio*. Milan: Rizzoli.

———. 2004a. *La forza della ragione*. Milan: Rizzoli.

———. 2004b. *Oriana Fallaci intervista sé stessa. L'Apocalisse*. Milan: Rizzoli.

Farah Elahi and Omar Khan. 2017. "Introduction: What Is Islamophobia?" In *Islamophobia: Still a Challenge for Us All*, by Farah Elahi and Omar Khan, 5–12. https://www.runnymedetrust .org/publications/islamophobia-still-a-challenge-for-us-all.

Farìas De Albuquerque, Fernanda, and Maurizio Jannelli. 1994. *Princesa. Dal Nordest a Rebibbia: Storia di una vita ai margini*. Rome: Sensibili alle Foglie.

———. 2013. *Princesa 20*. Edited by Ugo Fracassa and Anna Proto Pisani. http://www.princesa20.it.

Feltri, Vittorio. 2015. *Non abbiamo abbastanza paura: noi e L'Islam*. Milan: Mondadori.

Fortunato, Mario, and Methnani Salah. 1990. *Immigrato*. Rome: Theoria.

Frisina, Annalisa. 2007. *Giovani musulmani d'Italia*. Rome: Carocci.

Gardaphé, Fred, and Wenying Xu. 2007. "Introduction: Food in Multi-ethnic Literatures." *MELUS* 32 (4): 5–10.

Gerrand, Vivian. 2016. *Possible Spaces of Somali Belonging*. Melbourne: Melbourne University Publishing.

Ghazy, Ranza. 2007. *Oggi forse non ammazzo nessuno: storie minime di una giovane musulmana stranamente non terrorista*. Milan: Rizzoli.

Giuliani, Chiara. 2020. *Shirin Ramzanali Fazel*. https://modernlanguages.sas.ac.uk/research-centres/centre-study-contemporary-womens-writing/ccww-languages/italian.

Giuliani, Gaia. 2018. *Race, Nation and Gender in Modern Italy: Intersectional Representations in Visual Culture*. New York: Routledge.

Giuliani Caponetto, Rosetta. 2015. *Fascist Hybridities: Representations of Racial Mixing and Diaspora Cultures under Mussolini*. New York: Palgrave.

Gruber, Lilli. 2003. *I miei giorni a Baghdad*. Milan: RCS Libri.

Gustavsen, Bjørn. 2003. "New Forms of Knowledge Production and the Role of Action Research." *Action Research* 1 (2): 153–164.

Hunter, Ian. 1974. *Memory*. London: Penguin.

Huntington, Samuel P. 1997. *The Clash of Civilizations and the Remaking of World Order*. London: Simon & Schuster.

Jay, Paul. 2010. *Global Matters: The Transnational Turn in Literary Studies*. Ithaca, NY: Cornell University Press.

Kaha Mohamed Aden. 2010. *Fra-intendimenti*. Rome: Nottetempo.

Khaled Fouad Allam. 2011. *L'Islam spiegato ai leghisti*. Milan: Piemme.

———. 2004. *Lettera a un kamikaze*. Milan: Rizzoli.

Khouma, Pap. 2010. *I Was an Elephant Salesman: Adventures between Dakar, Paris, and Milan*. Translated by Rebecca Hopkins. Bloomington: Indiana University Press.

Kline, Elizabeth, and Barbara Williams. 2013. "Managing Users' Expectations of E-books." In *Adapting to E-books*, edited by William Miller and Rita M. Pellen, 249–255. London: Routledge.

Labanca, Nicola. 2002. *Oltremare. Storia dell'espansione coloniale italiana*. Bologna: il Mulino.

Lionnet, Françoise. 1989. *Autobiographical Voices: Race, Gender, Self-Portraiture*. Ithaca, NY: Cornell University Press.

Literatures Across Frontiers. 2015. "Translation Statistics from LAF." April 13. http://www.lit-across-frontiers.org/new-translation -statistics-from-laf/.

Lori, Laura. 2013. *Inchiostro d'Africa. La letteratura postcoloniale somala fra diaspora e identità*. Verona: Ombre Corte.

Mahalingappa, Laura, Terri Rodriguez, and Nihat Polat. 2017. *Supporting Muslim Students: A Guide to Understanding the Diverse Issues of Today's Classrooms*. Lanham, MD: Rowman & Littlefield.

Makaping, Geneviève. 2001. *Traiettorie di sguardi. E se gli altri foste voi?* Soveria Manelli: Rubbettino.

———. 2022a. *Reversing the Gaze: What If the Other Were You?* Edited by Simone Brioni. Translated by Giovanna Bellesia Contuzzi and Victoria Offredi Poletto. New Brunswick, NJ: Rutgers University Press.

———. 2022b. *Traiettorie di sguardi. E se gli altri foste voi?* Edited by Simone Brioni. Soveria Manelli: Rubbettino.

Marinetti, Filippo Tommaso. (1938) 2015. "Verso una imperiale arte culinaria. Inchiesta alla 'Scena Illustrata' (1938)." In *Cucina futurista. Manifesti teorici, menu e documenti*, edited by Guido Andrea Pautasso, 183–186. Milan: Abscondita.

———. 1989. *The Futurist Cookbook*. Edited by Lesley Chamberlain. Translated by Suzanne Brill. San Francisco: Bedford Arts.

Marinetti, Filippo Tommaso, and Fillìa. 1932. *Cucina Futurista*. Milan: Sonzogno.

Massari, Monica. 2006. *Islamofobia: la paura e l'islam*. Rome: Laterza.

Meneghelli, Donata. 2006. "Finzioni dell'io nella letteratura italiana della migrazione." *Narrativa* 28: 39–51.

Mengozzi, Chiara. 2013. *Narrazioni contese. Vent'anni di scritture italiane della migrazione*. Rome: Carocci.

Micheletti, Alessandro, and Saidou Moussa Ba. 1991. *La promessa di Hamadi*. Novara: De Agostini.

Mirzoeff, Nicholas, and Jack Halberstam. 2018. "Decolonize Media: Tactics, Manifestos, Histories." *Cinema Journal* 57 (4): 120–123.

Mohamed Issa Trunji. 2015. *Somalia: The Untold Story 1941–1969*. London: Looh Press.

Molinari, Maurizio. 2015. *Il Califfato del terrore: perché lo Stato Islamico minaccia l'Occidente*. Milan: Rizzoli.

Muhammad Ibn Ismail Bukhari. 1996. *The English Translation of Sahih Al Bukha- ri with the Arabic text*. 9 vols. Translated by Muhammad Muhsin Khan. Riyadh: Darussalam.

Morone, Antonio Maria. 2011. *L'ultima colonia. Come l'Italia è tornata in Africa 1950–1960*. Rome: Laterza.

———. 2018. "Racism: Meticci on the Eve of Colonial Downfall." In *The Horn of Africa and Italy: Colonial, Postcolonial and Transnational Cultural Encounters*, edited by Simone Brioni and Shimelis Bonsa Gulema, 167–192. Oxford: Peter Lang.

Nichols, Catherine. 2015. "Homme de Plume: What I Learned Sending My Novel Out under a Male Name." *Jezebel*, August 4. http://jezebel.com/homme-de-plume-what-i-learned-sending-my -novel-out-und-1720637627?utm_campaign=socialflow_jezebel _facebook&utm_source=jezebel_facebook&utm_medium =socialflow.

Nussbaum, Martha. 1995. "Objectification." *Philosophy and Public Affairs* 24 (4): 249–291.

Orsini, Francesca. 2006. "Canons and Rubber Boats: Oriana Fallaci and the 'Clash of Civilizations.'" *Interventions* 8 (3): 444–460.

Pagliara, Maria. 2001. *Il romanzo coloniale: tra imperialismo e rimorso*. Rome: Laterza.

Parati, Graziella. 2005. *Migration Italy: The Art of Talking Back in a Destination Culture*. Toronto: University of Toronto Press.

Pease, Donald. (1990) 1995. "Author." In *Critical Terms for Literary Studies*, edited Frank Lentricchia and Thomas McLaughlin, 105–117. Chicago: University of Chicago Press.

Pesarini, Angelica. 2018. "Dinamiche neocoloniali di genere, 'razza' e migrazione. L'universo femminile di Shirin Ramzanali Fazel in *Nuvole sull'equatore*." In *Donne e Sud. Percorsi nella letteratura italiana contemporanea*, edited by Ramona Onnis and Manuela Spinelli, 127–135. Florence: Franco Cesati.

Pinkus, Karen. 1995. *Bodily Regimes: Italian Advertising under Fascism*. Minneapolis: University of Minnesota Press.

Polezzi, Loredana. 2006. "Mixing Mother Tongues: Language, Narrative and the Spaces of Memory in Postcolonial Works by Italian Women Writers (Part 2)." *Romance Studies* 24 (3): 215–225.

Ponzanesi, Sandra. 2004. *Paradoxes of Postcolonial Culture: Contemporary Women Writers of the Indian and Afro-Italian Diaspora*. Albany: State University of New York Press.

———. 2014. *The Postcolonial Cultural Industry: Icons, Markets, Mythologies*. Basingstoke: Palgrave Macmillan.

Proglio, Gabriele. 2015. "Filigrana dell'immaginario. Cinema e razza al tempo della globalizzazione 1980–2001." In *Il colore della nazione*, edited by Gaia Giuliani, 61–75. Florence: Le Monnier.

———. 2020. *Islamofobia e razzismo. Media, discorsi pubblici e immaginario nella decostruzione dell'altro*. Turin: Edizioni SEB27.

Provoledo, Elisabetta. 2007. "Randa Ghazy: A Chick-Lit Novelist with a Multi-ethnic Tale." *New York Times*, May 29.

Prunetti, Alberto. 2016. "Per una critica del cervellone in fuga." *Il lavoro culturale*, April 1. http://www.lavoroculturale.org/critica-del-cervellone-fuga-un-punto-vista-working-class/.

Quirico, Domenico. 2015. *Il grande califfato*. Milan: Neri Pozza.

Ranzini, Paola, Anna Proto Pisani, and Olivier Favier, eds. 2016. *Les littératures de la Corne de l'Afrique. Regards croisés*. Paris: Karthala.

Redazione La Stampa. 2010. "Il dilemma di Silvio: Far digerire a Bossi gli ascari meridionali." *La Stampa*, September 15. http://www.lastampa.it/2010/09/15/italia/politica/il-dilemma-di-silvio-far-digerire-a-bossi-gli-ascari-meridionali-JVawEqC5b8VewQ7EHWENBI/pagina.html.

Redazione La Repubblica. 2010. "Silvio guida la caccia agli ascari." *La Repubblica*, September 16. http://ricerca.repubblica.it/repubblica/archivio/repubblica/2010/09/16/silvio-guida-la-caccia-agli-ascari.html.

Remarque Koutonin, Mawuna. 2015. "Why Are White People Expats When the Rest of Us Are Immigrants?" *Guardian*, March 13. https://www.theguardian.com/global-development-professionals-network/2015/mar/13/white-people-expats-immigrants-migration.

Resistenze in Cirenaica. 2016a. *I quaderni di Cirene n. 1*. Bologna: Autoproduzioni Senza Blackjack.

———. 2016b. *I quaderni di Cirene n. 2*. Bologna: Autoproduzioni Senza Blackjack.

Ribka Sibhatu. 1993. *Aulò. Canto-Poesia dell'Eritrea*. Rome: Sinnos.

Romano, Rose. 2016a. *Neither Seen or Heard*. United Kingdom: CreateSpace.

———. 2016b. *You'll Never Have Me Like You Want Me*. United Kingdom: CreateSpace.

Romeo, Caterina. 2018. *Riscrivere la nazione. La letteratura italiana postcoloniale*. Milan: Mondadori.

Ruba Salih. 1998. *Musulmane Rivelate. Donne, Islam, Modernità*. Rome: Carocci.

Scarpellini, Emanuela. 2012. *A tavola! Gli italiani in 7 pranzi*. Rome: Laterza.

Scego, Igiaba. 2005. "Dismatria." In *Pecore nere*, edited by Flavia Capitani and Emanuele Coen, 5–21. Rome: Laterza.

———. 2008. *Oltre Babilonia*. Rome: Donzelli.

———. 2015. "La vera storia di Faccetta Nera." *Internazionale*, August 6. http://www.internazionale.it/opinione/igiaba-scego /2015/08/06/faccetta-nera-razzismo.

Scego, Igiaba, and Shirin Ramzanali Fazel. 2008. "Scrittrice Nomade." *Internazionale*, February 22, 60.

Sciortino, Giuseppe. 2002. "Islamofobia all'italiana." *Polis* 16 (1): 103–123.

Shirin Ramzanali Fazel. 1994. *Lontano da Mogadiscio*. Rome: Datanews.

———. 2010. *Nuvole sull'equatore. Gli italiani dimenticati. Una storia.* Cuneo: Nerosubianco.

———. 2013. *Lontano da Mogadiscio / Far from Mogadishu*. Milan: Laurana.

———. 2015. "Foggy Dreams under the Sun Sunshine." In *Moments in Time*, edited by Writers Without Borders, 56. New York: Lulu.

———. 2017a. *Clouds over the Equator: The Forgotten Italians*. Scotts Valley, CA: CreateSpace.

———. 2017b. *Far from Mogadishu*. Scotts Valley, CA: CreateSpace.

———. 2017c. *Lontano da Mogadiscio*. Scotts Valley, CA: CreateSpace.

———. 2017d. *Nuvole sull'equatore. Gli italiani dimenticati. Una storia.* Scotts Valley, CA: CreateSpace.

———. 2017e. *Wings*. Scotts Valley, CA: CreateSpace.

———. 2020a. *I Suckled Sweetness: Poems*. Scotts Valley, CA: CreateSpace.

———. 2020b. "Io e l'Islam." In *Scrivere di Islam: Raccontare la Diaspora*, by Simone Brioni and Shirin Ramzanali Fazel, 37–92. Venice: Cà Foscari Edizioni.

———. 2021. "My Beloved Stepmother." In *Italy Is Out*, by Mario Badagliacca with Derek Duncan, 51. Liverpool: Liverpool University Press.

———. 2022a. "Shirin Ramzanali Fazel." In *Alibi. Prima antologia di poesia italiana nel Regno Unito*, edited by Marta Arnaldi and Luca Paci, 232–252. Rome: Ensemble.

———. 2022b. "Shirin Ramzanali Fazel." In *Tempo: Excursion in 21st Century Italian Poetry*, edited by Luca Paci, 103–119. Cardigan: Parthian.

Soules, Aline. 2013. "New Types of E-books, E-book Issues and Implications for the Future." In *Adapting to E-books*, edited by William Miller and Rita M. Pellen, 207–228. London: Routledge.

Sumaya Abdel Qader. 2019. *Quello che abbiamo in testa*. Milan: Mondadori.

Thomassen, Bjørn. 2010. "'Second Generation Immigrants' or 'Italians with Immigrant Parents'? Italian and European Perspectives on Immigrants and Their Children." *Bulletin of Italian Politics* 2: 21–44.

Tirabassi, Maddalena, and Alvise Del Prà. 2014. *La meglio Italia. Le mobilità italiane nel XXI secolo*. Turin: Accademia University Press.

Tripodi, Paolo. 1999. *The Colonial Legacy in Somalia. Rome and Mogadishu: From Colonial Administration to Operation Restore Hope*. London: Palgrave Macmillan.

Venturini, Monica. 2010. "Incontro con Shirin Ramzanali Fazel: tra Italia e Somalia." In *Controcànone—Per una cartografia della scrittura coloniale e post-coloniale italiana*, edited by Monica Venturini, 137–146. Rome: Aracne.

Vertovec, Steven. 2009. *Transnationalism*. London: Routledge.

Wadia, Laila. 2016. *Kitchen Sutra. The Love of Language, the Language of Love. L'amore del linguaggio il linguaggio dell'amore*. United Kingdom: Amazon.

Wall, Georgia, and Naomi Wells. 2020. "Emplaced and Embodied Encounters: Methodological Reflections on Transcultural Research in Contexts of Italian Migration." *Modern Italy* 25 (2): 113–129.

Welch, Rhiannon Noel. 2010. "Intimate Truth and (Post)colonial Knowledge in Shirin Ramzanali Fazel's Lontano da Mogadiscio." In *National Belongings: Hybridity in Italian Colonial and Postcolonial Studies*, edited by Jaqueline Andall and Derek Duncan, 215–233. Oxford: Peter Lang.

Wells, Naomi, et al. 2019. "Ethnography and Modern Languages." *Modern Languages Open* 1 (1). http://doi.org/10.3828/mlo .v0i0.242.

Wood, Sharon. 2006. "A 'Quattro Mani': Collaboration in Italian Immigrant Literature." In *Collaboration in the Arts from the Middle Ages to the Present*, edited by Sara Bigliazzi and Sharon Wood, 151–162. Aldershot: Ashgate.

Wright, John. 2010. "Mussolini, Libya and the Sword of Islam." In *Italian Colonialism*, edited by Ruth Ben-Ghiat and Mia Fuller, 121–130. New York: Palgrave Macmillan.

Wu Ming. 2016. "Il razzismo italiano e i fantasmi del deserto, ovvero: 20 sfondoni di Maurizio Molinari (e una nota su Dacia Maraini)." *Giap!*, January 13. http://www.wumingfoundation .com/giap/?p=23250.

Wu Ming 1. 2008. "New Italian Epic 2.0. Memorandum 1993–2008. Letteratura, sguardo obliquo, ritorno al futuro." Wu Ming Foundation. https://www.wumingfoundation.com/italiano /WM1_saggio_sul_new_italian_epic.pdf.

Wu Ming 2 and Antar Mohamed. 2012. *Timira. Romanzo meticcio*. Turin: Einaudi.

Zubair 'Ali Za'i, ed. 2007. *Jami' at-Tirmidhi*. Translated by Abu Khaliyl. Houston: Dar-us-Salam Publications.

## Websites

La molisana. "N. 25 Abissine Rigate." http://www.lamolisana.it /abissinerigate-25.

La molisana. "N.68 Tripoline." http://www.lamolisana.it/francesca/
    -/asset_publisher/LOWGCPh5ipLi/content/n-68-tripoline
    /maximized.

Laurana. "Reloaded." http://www.laurana.it/index.php.

Open DDB. http://www.openddb.com.

Transnationalizing Modern Languages. http://www.transnational
    modernlanguages.ac.uk.

# About the Contributors

SHIRIN RAMZANALI FAZEL is an Italian writer of Somali and Pakistani origins. Shirin was born in Mogadishu, Somalia, where she attended Italian schools. In 1971, she left her country and arrived in Novara, Italy. Shirin has lived in several countries, including Zambia, the United States, Kenya, Saudi Arabia, and Tunisia. She currently lives in Birmingham, United Kingdom. Her first novel, *Lontano da Mogadiscio*, is considered a milestone of Italian postcolonial literature, and it describes her experience of migration to Italy and the effects of Italian colonialism in her native country. Shirin's second novel, *Nuvole sull'Equatore*, fleshes out the issue of *meticciato* and race discrimination, a crude legacy of the Italian colonial government. *Lontano da Mogadiscio / Far from Mogadishu*, an extended and bilingual version of the 1994 edition, was published in 2013 as an e-book. In 2016, the English translation appeared in printed form. Her publications also include the collection of poems *Wings* (2017) and *I Suckled Sweetness* (2020). Shirin was part of the advisory board of the Arts and Humanities Research Council–funded project Transnationalizing Modern Languages (http://www.transnationalmodernlanguages.ac.uk).

SIMONE BRIONI is an associate professor in the Department of English at Stony Brook University and affiliated faculty in the Department of Africana Studies and the Department of Women's, Gender and Sexuality Studies. His research focuses on the literary and cinematographic representation and self-representation of migrants. He has edited Geneviève Makaping's *Reversing the Gaze: What If the Other Were You?* (Rutgers University Press, 2023), which is also included in the Other Voices of Italy series.